New Perspectives on

PRESENTATION CONCEPTS

BEVERLY B. ZIMMERMAN
Brigham Young University

COURSE
TECHNOLOGY
THOMSON LEARNING

Australia • Canada • Mexico • Singapore • Spain • United Kingdom • United States

New Perspectives on Presentation Concepts is published by Course Technology.

Managing Editor	Greg Donald
Senior Editor	Donna Gridley
Series Technology Editor	Rachel A. Crapser
Product Manager	Catherine V. Donaldson
Associate Product Manager	Melissa Dezotell
Editorial Assistant	Rosa Maria Rogers
Developmental Editor	Rose Marie Kuebbing
Production Editor	Christine Spillett
Text Designer	Meral Dabcovich
Cover Designer	Douglas Goodman

© 2001 by Course Technology, a division of Thomson Learning

For more information contact:

Course Technology
25 Thomson Place
Boston, MA 02210
Or find us on the World Wide Web at: http://www.course.com

For permission to use material from this text or product, contact us by

■ Web: www.thomsonrights.com
■ Phone: 1-800-730-2214
■ Fax: 1-800-730-2215

ISBN 0-619-01978-6

Printed in the United States of America

1 2 3 4 5 6 7 8 9 10   BM 05 04 03 02 01

PREFACE

The New Perspectives Series

About New Perspectives

Course Technology's **New Perspectives Series** is an integrated system of instruction that combines text and technology products to teach computer concepts, the Internet, and microcomputer applications. Users consistently praise this series for innovative pedagogy, use of interactive technology, creativity, accuracy, and supportive and engaging style.

How is the New Perspectives Series different from other series?

The **New Perspectives Series** distinguishes itself by **innovative technology**, from the renowned Course Labs to the state-of-the-art multimedia that is integrated with our Concepts texts. Other distinguishing features include **sound instructional design, proven pedagogy**, and **consistent quality**. Each tutorial has students learn features in the context of solving a realistic case problem rather than simply learning a laundry list of features. With the **New Perspectives Series**, instructors report that students have a complete, integrative learning experience that stays with them. They credit this high retention and competency to the fact that this series incorporates critical thinking and problem-solving with computer skills mastery. In addition, we work hard to ensure accuracy by using a multi-step quality assurance process during all stages of development. Instructors focus on teaching and students spend more time learning.

What course is this book appropriate for?

New Perspectives on Presentation Concepts can be used in any course in which you want students to learn all the most important topics of how to give oral presentations, including planning a presentation, determining the purpose and outcomes for a presentation, analyzing the audience and situation for a presentation, selecting an appropriate medium, organizing a presentation, using effective visuals, choosing an appropriate delivery method, and delivering a presentation. It is particularly recommended for a short course or part of a longer course on giving formal and informal presentations. It would also work well as part of a course on computer presentations, such as Microsoft PowerPoint.

Proven Pedagogy

Tutorial Case Each tutorial begins with a problem presented in a case that is meaningful to students. The case turns the task of learning how to use an application into a problem-solving process.

45-minute Sessions Each tutorial is divided into sessions that can be completed in about 45 minutes to an hour. Sessions allow instructors to more accurately allocate time in their syllabus, and students to better manage their own study time.

Step-by-Step Methodology We make sure students can differentiate between what they are to *do* and what they are to *read*. Through numbered steps—clearly identified by a gray shaded background—students are constantly guided in solving the case problem. In addition, the numerous screen shots with callouts direct students' attention to what they should look at on the screen.

TROUBLE? | **TROUBLE? Paragraphs** These paragraphs anticipate the mistakes or problems that students may have and help them continue with the tutorial.

Tutorial Tips Page This page, following the Table of Contents, offers students suggestions on how to effectively plan their study and lab time, what to do when they make a mistake, and how to use the Reference Windows, MOUS grids, Quick Checks, and other features of the New Perspectives series.

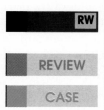

Quick Check Questions Each session concludes with meaningful, conceptual Quick Check questions that test students' understanding of what they learned in the session. Answers to the Quick Check questions are provided at the end of each tutorial.

Reference Windows are succinct summaries of the most important tasks covered in a tutorial and they preview actions students will perform in the steps to follow.

End-of-Tutorial Review Assignments and Case Problems Review Assignments provide students with additional hands-on practice of the skills they learned in the tutorial using the same case presented in the tutorial. These Assignments are followed by three to four Case Problems that have approximately the same scope as the tutorial case but use a different scenario.

New Perspectives on Presentation Concepts Instructor's Resource Kit contains:
- Electronic Instructor's Manual in Word 97 format
- Course Test Manager Testbank
- Course Test Manager Engine
- Figure Files
- Sample Syllabus

These supplements come on CD-ROM. If you don't have access to a CD-ROM drive, contact your Course Technology customer service representative for more information.

More innovative technology

Course CBT

Enhance your students' Office 2000 classroom learning experience with self-paced computer-based training on CD-ROM. Course CBT engages students with interactive multimedia and hands-on simulations that reinforce and complement the concepts and skills covered in the textbook. All the content is aligned with the MOUS (Microsoft Office User Specialist) program, making it a great preparation tool for the certification exams. Course CBT also includes extensive pre- and post-assessments that test students' mastery of skills. These pre- and post-assessments automatically generate a "custom learning path" through the course that highlights only the topics students need help with.

Skills Assessment Manager (SAM)

How well do your students *really* know Microsoft Office? SAM is a performance-based testing program that measures students' proficiency in Microsoft Office 2000. SAM is available for Office 2000 in either a live or simulated environment. You can use SAM to place students into or out of courses, monitor their performance throughout a course, and help prepare them for the MOUS certification exams.

CyberClass

CyberClass is a Web-based tool designed for on-campus or distance learning. Use it to enhance how you currently run your class by posting assignments and your course syllabus or holding online office hours. Or, use it for your distance learning course, and offer mini-lectures, conduct online discussion groups, or give your mid-term exam. For more information, visit our Web site at: **www.course.com/products/cyberclass/index.html.**

WebCT

WebCT is a tool used to create Web-based educational environments and also uses WWW browsers as the interface for the course-building environment. The site is hosted on your school campus, allowing complete control over the information. WebCT has its own internal communication system, offering internal e-mail, a Bulletin Board, and a Chat room. Course Technology offers pre-existing supplemental information to help in your WebCT class creation, such as a suggested Syllabus, Lecture Notes, Figures in the Book/Course Presenter, Student Downloads, and Test Banks in which you can schedule an exam, create reports, and more.

Acknowledgments

The author would like to thank the following reviewers for their valuable feedback on this project: Janette Moody, The Citadel; and Linda Reis, Garland County Community College. Also special thanks goes to Melissa Dezotell, Associate Product Manager; Christine Spillett, Production Editor; Rachel Crapser, Series Technology Editor; Greg Donald, Managing Editor; Donna Gridley, Senior Editor; Catherine Donaldson, Product Manager; John Bosco, Quality Assurance Project Leader; and the staff at GEX. Thank you all for your expertise, enthusiasm, and vision for this book. Finally, I would like to thank Rose Marie Kuebbing, my developmental editor, for her expert assistance and friendly support.

Beverly B. Zimmerman

TABLE OF CONTENTS

Reference **Window**

Tutorial Tips

These tutorials will help you learn about presentation skills. The tutorials are designed to be worked through at a computer. Each tutorial is divided into sessions. Watch for the session headings, such as Session 1.1 and Session 1.2. Each session is designed to be completed in about 45 minutes, but take as much time as you need. It's also a good idea to take a break between sessions.

To use the tutorials effectively, read the following questions and answers before you begin.

Where do I start?

Each tutorial begins with a case, which sets the scene for the tutorial and gives you background information to help you understand what you will be doing. Read the case before you go to the lab. In the lab, begin with the first session of a tutorial.

How do I know what to do on the computer?

Each session contains steps that you will perform to learn how to use presentation skills. Read the text that introduces each series of steps. The steps you need to do at a computer are numbered and are set against a shaded background. Read each step carefully and completely before you try it.

What if I make a mistake?

Don't worry about making mistakes—they are part of the learning process. Paragraphs labeled "TROUBLE?" identify common problems and explain how to get back on track. Follow the steps in a TROUBLE? paragraph only if you are having the problem described. If you run into other problems:

- Carefully consider the current state of your system, the position of the pointer, and any messages on the screen.

- Complete the sentence, "Now I want to…" Be specific, because identifying your goal will help you rethink the steps you need to take to reach that goal.

- If you are working on a particular piece of software, consult the Help system.

- If the suggestions above don't solve your problem, consult your technical support person for assistance.

How do I use the Reference Windows?

Reference Windows summarize the procedures you will learn in the tutorial steps. Do not complete the actions in the Reference Windows when you are working through the tutorial. Instead, refer to the Reference Windows while you are working on the assignments at the end of the tutorial.

How can I test my understanding of the material I learned in the tutorial?

At the end of each session, you can answer the Quick Check questions. The answers for the Quick Checks are at the end of that tutorial.

After you have completed the entire tutorial, you should complete the Review Assignments and Case Problems. They are carefully structured so that you will review what you have learned and then apply your knowledge to new situations.

What if I can't remember how to do something?

Before you begin the tutorials, you should know the basics about your computer's operating system. You should also know how to use the menus, dialog boxes, Help system, and My Computer.

Now that you've read the Tutorial Tips, you are ready to begin.

New Perspectives on

PRESENTATION CONCEPTS

OBJECTIVES

In this tutorial you will:

- Write a statement of purpose for your presentation

- Analyze the needs and expectations of your audience

- Assess the situation in which you'll give your presentation

- Select an appropriate medium for your presentation

- Limit your topic to provide focus

- Outline the general organization of a presentation

- Develop an effective introduction, body, and conclusion

PLANNING AND DEVELOPING YOUR PRESENTATION

Presentations for Youth Essential Services (YES!), a Nonprofit Service Agency

Giving Presentations for YES!

As a student at Rocky Mountain State College, you recently obtained an internship with Youth Essential Services (YES!), a private, nonprofit organization serving school-aged children with physical and mental disabilities in the Colorado Springs area. The mission of YES! is to provide developmentally challenged youth with training and motivational programs to help them function effectively in society. Presently, the organization serves between 1100 and 1300 young people each month.

Kenna McNaughton, executive director of YES!, says that you'll make many oral presentations as part of your internship. Some of these presentations will be brief and informal, such as communicating pertinent information to the YES! staff, or providing training to volunteers. Other presentations will be lengthy and formal, such as reporting on the status of programs to the Board of Directors, or requesting funds from potential donors. Sometimes you'll need to convey your entire message in an oral format; other times your presentation might supplement a written document, such as a financial statement or a wrap-up report for a successful project. Sometimes you'll give your presentation as part of a group or team; other times you'll give your presentation alone. The success of your internship—and of many of the organization's programs—will depend upon the quality of your presentations.

SESSION 1.1

In this session, you'll learn the skills for planning a presentation: determining the purpose of your presentation, analyzing the needs and expectations of your audience or listeners, assessing the situation (environment) for your presentation, and choosing an appropriate medium. Regardless of the type of presentation you give, its effectiveness will be determined by how well you plan your presentation.

Planning Your Presentation

Plan your oral presentation the same way you would plan a written document—consider your purpose, audience, and situation. Oral presentations, however, differ from written documents in the demands placed upon your audience, so you'll need to apply special techniques to ensure a successful presentation.

Planning a presentation in advance will improve the quality of your presentation, make it more effective and enjoyable, and, in the long run, save you time and effort. As you plan your presentation, you should determine why you're giving the presentation, who will be listening to the presentation, and where the presentation will take place.

Figure 1-1	PLANNING SAVES TIME

Specific questions you should ask yourself about the presentation include:

- What is the purpose of this presentation?
- What type of presentation do I need to give?
- Who is the audience for my presentation, and what do they need and expect?
- What is the situation (location and setting) for my presentation?
- What is the most appropriate media for my presentation?

Answering these questions will help you create a more effective presentation, and will enable you to feel confident in presenting your ideas. The following sections will help you answer these questions in planning your presentation.

Determining the Purpose of Your Presentation

■ Your purpose in giving a presentation will vary according to each particular situation, so the best way to determine your purpose is to ask yourself why you're giving this presentation and what you expect to accomplish. Common purposes for giving presentations include to inform, to persuade, and to demonstrate or train. We'll now consider these types of presentations.

Giving Informative Presentations

Informative presentations provide your audience with background information, knowledge, and specific details about a topic that enable them to make informed decisions, form attitudes, or increase their expertise on a topic.

Examples of informative presentations include:

■ Academic or professional conference presentations

■ Briefings on the status of projects

■ Reviews or evaluations of products and services

■ Reports at company meetings

■ Luncheon or dinner speeches

■ Informal symposia

Figure 1-2	PROVIDE BACKGROUND AND DETAILS

Informative presentations can address a wide range of topics and are given to a wide range of audiences. For example, you might want to educate students at Rocky Mountain State College about the goals and programs of YES!, or you might want to inform YES! staff members about plans for next month's sports activity. Or, you might want to tell parents of youth participating in YES!-sponsored activities about the organization of the Board of Directors. Your main goal in each instance is to provide useful and relevant information to your intended audience.

Giving Persuasive Presentations

Although every presentation involves influencing an audience to listen and be interested in a specific topic, some presentations are more persuasive than others. Presentations with the specific goal of persuasion attempt to influence how an audience feels or acts regarding a particular position or plan.

Examples of persuasive presentations include:

- Recommendations
- Sales presentations
- Action plans and strategy sessions
- Motivational presentations

| Figure 1-3 | INFLUENCE YOUR AUDIENCE |

Persuasive presentations also cover a wide range of topics and are given to a wide range of audiences. In addition, persuasive presentations are usually designed as balanced arguments involving logical as well as emotional reasons for supporting an action or viewpoint. For example, you might want to persuade students at Rocky Mountain State College to volunteer their time in community service. Or, you might want to recommend a particular fundraising activity to YES! administrators. Or, you might want to motivate parents of YES! participants to apply for additional services for their children. Your goal in each of these persuasive presentations is to convince your audience to accept a particular plan or point of view.

Giving Demonstrations or Training Presentations

Audiences attend demonstrations to see how something works or to understand a process or procedure. Examples of demonstration presentations include:

- Overviews of products and services
- Software demonstrations
- Process explanations

For example, you might want to demonstrate to volunteers from Rocky Mountain State College how to give encouragement and support to handicapped youth at athletic events. Or, you might want to show YES! staff members how the new accounting software handles reimbursements. Or, you might want to show parents of YES! participants how to fill out a transportation release form. In each of these presentations, your goal is to show how something works so your audience understands the process.

Training presentations provide audiences with an opportunity to learn new skills, or to educate themselves on how to perform a task, such as how to operate a piece of equipment. Training presentations usually differ from demonstrations by providing listeners with hands-on experience, practice, and feedback, so they can correct their mistakes and improve their performances. Examples of training presentations include:

- Employee orientation (completing job tasks such as running the copy machine)
- Seminars and workshops
- Educational classes and courses

| Figure 1-4 | SHOW HOW TO PERFORM A TASK |

For example, you might want to provide training to volunteers from Rocky Mountain State College on how to manage conflict during team sports. Or, you might want to present a seminar to the YES! staff on how to write an effective grant proposal. Or, you might want to teach parents of YES! participants how to help their children with basic life skills, such as counting money. In all of these presentations, your goal is to assist your audience in learning and practicing new abilities and skills.

Sometimes you may have more than one purpose for your presentation. For instance, you need to inform the YES! staff of the newly revised policy on transporting participants to organized activities. In addition to explaining the new policy, you'll need to persuade your co-workers of the importance of following the new guidelines. You might also need to answer any questions they have about how to implement certain aspects of the policy.

Having too many purposes can complicate your presentation and keep you from focusing on the specific needs of your audience. For that reason, you should try to limit your presentation to one main purpose, and one or two secondary purposes.

REFERENCE   WINDOW   **RW**

<u>Purposes for Giving Presentations</u>

Type of Presentation	Goal of Presentation	Examples
Informative	Present facts and details	Academic or professional conferences, status reports, briefings, reviews of products and services, luncheon or dinner speeches, informal symposia
Persuasive	Influence feelings or actions	Recommendation reports, sales presentations, action plans and strategy sessions, motivational presentations
Demonstrations or Training	Show how something works; provide practice and feedback	Overviews of products and services, software demos, process explanations, employee orientation, seminars and workshops, educational courses

---

In addition to determining your purpose for a presentation, you should also consider the needs of your audience. Effective presentations are those that enable listeners to achieve their goals. We will now consider how to determine what the audience should gain or learn from your presentation.

Determining the Outcome of Your Presentation

Your goal in giving a presentation should be to help your listeners understand, retain, and use the information you present. So, you should determine what you want to happen as a result of your presentation. Focusing on the outcome of your presentation—what you want your listeners to think or do after listening to your message—forces you to make your presentation more audience-oriented. By addressing the needs of your listeners, you'll worry less about yourself and more about how to make your presentation effective for your audience.

Writing Purpose and Outcome Statements

Writing down the purpose and outcome of your presentation helps you to analyze what the presentation will involve, and enables you to create a more effective presentation. When you write down the purpose and desired outcomes of your presentation, you should use just two or three sentences. A good statement of your purpose and desired outcomes helps you later as you write the introduction and conclusion for your presentation.

Consider the following examples of purpose statements and outcomes:

- Purpose: To demonstrate the newly purchased arm pads and leg braces for moderately handicapped youth participating in YES! activities. Outcomes: Staff members will understand that the new equipment can decrease the number of injuries to participants. Staff members will want to use the new equipment at next month's field day.

- Purpose: To inform teachers of intellectually handicapped children in the community about the goals and programs of YES! Outcomes: Teachers will want eligible students to participate in YES! sponsored activities.

Teachers will know the eligibility criteria for participation, and how to refer their students to our organization.

In both of these examples, the presenter stated a specific purpose with specific outcomes.

REFERENCE WINDOW | RW

Questions for Determining Your Purpose and Outcomes
- Why am I giving this presentation?
- What is the primary purpose of this presentation?
- What are the secondary purposes of this presentation?
- What should the audience know or do as a result of this presentation?

Your supervisor, Kenna, asks you to give a presentation about YES! to student leaders at Rocky Mountain State College. Your written purpose might be: To inform student leaders of the goals and programs of YES! Your written outcome might be: Student leaders will want to create an official partnership between YES! and Rocky Mountain State College so that students can receive course credit for their volunteer work with the agency.

Figure 1.5 provides a basic worksheet for helping you determine the purpose and outcomes of this and other presentations.

| Figure 1-5 | PURPOSE AND OUTCOMES WORKSHEET |

Purpose and Outcomes
Worksheet

Why are you giving this presentation?
_____
_____
_____

What is the primary purpose of your presentation? Check one and explain it.
 ☐ Provide useful and relevant facts and details
_____
_____

 ☐ Persuade or influence how audience feels or acts
_____
_____

 ☐ Show how something works or demonstrate a procedure
_____
_____

 ☐ Provide hands-on experience, practice, and feedback
_____
_____

What are the secondary purposes for your presentation? Check and explain all that apply.
 ☐ Provide useful and relevant facts and details
_____

 ☐ Persuade or influence how audience feels or acts
_____

 ☐ Show how something works or demonstrate a procedure
_____

 ☐ Provide hands-on experience, practice, and feedback
_____

 ☐ Other

What should the audience know, feel, or do as a result of your presentation?
_____
_____
_____

What other outcomes are there for your presentation?
_____
_____
_____

Next you'll analyze what your audience will need and expect from your presentation.

Analyzing **Your Audience's Needs and Expectations**

The more you know about your listeners, the more you'll be able to adapt your presentation to their needs. By putting yourself in your listeners' shoes, you'll be able to visualize your audience as more than just a group of passive listeners, and anticipate what they need and expect from your presentation. Anticipating the needs of your audience will also increase the chances that your audience will react favorably to your presentation.

When you give a presentation to YES! employees, your audience consists of professionals, such as counselors, therapists, and support staff. Audiences in these categories typically are interested in specifics related to their job functions, as well as how your desired outcomes will impact their workload, fulfill their goals and objectives, and affect their budget. In addition, YES! coworkers usually want a less formal presentation than audiences outside your organization.

When you give your presentation at Rocky Mountain State College, your audience will consist of other students and interested faculty and administrators. They will expect to learn: how student involvement in community service benefits the campus community; how community service experiences can supplement what students learn in the classroom; how a partnership between YES! and Rocky Mountain State College would function; and what the administrative costs would be for the university.

Other characteristics of your audience that you'll want to consider include demographic features such as age, gender, level of education, and familiarity with your topic.

Figure 1-6	ADAPT TO THE NEEDS OF YOUR AUDIENCE

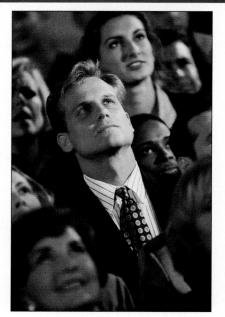

Examples of how demographic characteristics can affect your presentations include:

- **Age:** People of different age groups may vary in terms of attention span and the way they relate to examples. A presentation on the educational impact of student involvement in community service would be appropriate for college students, but probably not for elementary-school students. Moreover, young children have shorter attention spans and generally can't sit for as long as adults. Presentations to young children should be divided into short sessions interspersed with physical activity.

- **Gender:** It's important to fairly represent both genders by avoiding male pronouns (he, his) to represent both sexes, and by using examples that show both men and women performing all jobs at work and at home.

- **Education:** Audiences with specialized training expect examples that use terms and concepts from their field. Audiences with more education expect a higher level of technicality than audiences with less education.

- **Familiarity with the topic:** Audiences familiar with your topic won't need as many definitions and explanations as audiences not familiar with your topic.

In addition to analyzing general features and characteristics of your audience, you should also consider how your audience will use the information that you present. YES! administrators attending a presentation on potential fundraising activities need to know how much money other organizations have raised, and how much the fundraising activity itself would cost, in order to estimate their net profit.

Understanding the needs and expectations of your audience helps you adapt the content of your presentation to a particular audience, and enables you to address their concerns. By anticipating questions your listeners might ask about your topic, you can address those questions and concerns in your presentation. Finally, understanding the needs and concerns of your audience assures that your presentation is useful, interesting, and relevant.

REFERENCE WINDOW   **RW**

Questions for Analyzing Your Audience

- Who will be listening to my presentation (peers, superiors, subordinates, strangers)?
- What do they expect me to talk about?
- What general characteristics do I know about the audience (age, gender, education level, knowledge of the topic)?
- What do they need to know about the topic (general background or overview, details, cost estimates)?
- How will my listeners use this information (make decisions, perform a task)?
- What are my audience's major concerns or objections (too expensive, too difficult)?
- What do I want my audience to think, know, or do as a result of this presentation?

In your presentation about YES!, you realize that your audience will be your peers. They will vary in their experience with your topic, but most of them will be familiar with volunteerism. The biggest concern of college students is that involvement in service activities with YES! might be too time-consuming. You'll need to address that concern in your presentation.

Figure 1.7 provides a basic worksheet for helping you analyze the needs and expectations of your audience for this and other presentations.

Figure 1-7   **AUDIENCE ANALYSIS WORKSHEET**

Audience Analysis Worksheet

Who will be listening to your presentation? Check all that apply.
- ☐ Peers
- ☐ Superiors
- ☐ Subordinates
- ☐ Strangers

What do they expect you to talk about?
_____
_____

What general characteristics do you know about the audience?
- Age _____
- Gender _____
- Education _____
- Experience with topic _____
- Other _____

What does your audience need to know about the topic? Check and explain all that apply.
- ☐ General background or overview _____
- ☐ Details _____
- ☐ Cost estimates _____
- ☐ Other _____

How will your listeners use this information? Check and explain all that apply.
- ☐ Make decisions _____
- ☐ Perform a task _____
- ☐ Form an opinion _____
- ☐ Increase understanding _____
- ☐ Other _____

What are your audience's biggest concerns or objections? Check and explain all that apply.
- ☐ Too expensive _____
- ☐ Too difficult _____
- ☐ Other _____

What do you want your audience to think, know, or do as a result of this presentation?
_____
_____
_____

Assessing the Situation for Your Presentation

Many of your presentations will involve speaking on the same subject to different audiences and in different settings. Planning an effective presentation will be a matter of learning to adapt your content to each unique situation. The more you know about the circumstances, the better you can adapt your presentation to different audiences.

Probably the most important aspect to consider is how much time you'll have, and whether someone else will speak before or after you. Speaking with others means you'll have to watch your time closely so you don't infringe on someone else's time. It can also mean that you'll have to cut your presentation short because someone has used part of your time. Even if you're the sole speaker, it's wise to make back-up plans in case your time limit changes just before you speak.

Figure 1-8   SETTING AND LOCATIONS AFFECT EXPECTATIONS

The setting for a presentation can affect audience expectations, and hence will dictate the appropriate level of formality. That's why it's important to know where your presentation will occur, including the size and shape of the room, and the seating arrangement. The small conference room with a round table and moveable chairs at YES! headquarters would call for a much more informal presentation than the large rectangular lecture hall with fixed seating at Rocky Mountain State College.

You'll also need to adapt your presentation according to the size of your audience. Four or five co-workers at YES! would probably expect to be able to interrupt your presentation and ask questions or express their own views, versus the expectations of a large audience at Rocky Mountain State College. The setting for your presentation and size of your audience also influence the type of medium you can use, and the size of your visuals. Students in large rooms often sit toward the back of the room, far away from your visuals. You will need to increase the size of your visuals in your presentation at Rocky Mountain State College, or use an overhead, slide, or computer projection system. On the other hand, if your audience at YES! is fewer than ten people, you might be able to use a laptop computer screen for your visuals.

REFERENCE WINDOW   **RW**

Questions For Analyzing Your Presentation Situation
- How much time will I have for my presentation?
- Will I be speaking alone or with other people?
- How large will the audience be?
- How formal or informal will the setting be?
- What will the room be like, and how will it be arranged?
- What equipment will be available for my presentation (chalkboard, overhead projector, slide projector, computer projection system)?
- Do I have the skills to operate available equipment?
- Who will be available to assist me in case of an equipment failure?
- How much time will I have to set up for my presentation?
- What other aspects must I consider (temperature, extraneous noises)?
- Who will be available to assist me with room temperature, lights, or extraneous noise problems?
- How should I introduce myself and my qualifications?

Now you need to decide what kind of media you'll use in your presentation.

Selecting Appropriate Media

As you plan your presentation, you'll need to select the media you'll use to support and clarify your presentation. Media commonly used for oral presentations include:

- Chalkboard
- Whiteboard
- Notepad and easel
- Flip chart
- Posters
- Black-and-white or color overheads
- Handouts
- 35mm slides
- Computer-projected visuals, such as PowerPoint slides.

In selecting appropriate media for your presentation, it's important to fit the media to your particular purpose, audience, and situation. Every medium allows you to provide support for the points you'll make in your presentation, and help your audience see and hear your ideas. Each medium, however, has its own strengths and limitations. We'll consider those now.

Using a Chalkboard, Whiteboard, or Notepad

Chalkboards, whiteboards, or large paper notepads work well for small meetings and informal discussions, and are especially helpful in stressing important points from your presentation, or in recording comments from the audience. These media usually require little advance preparation, other than bringing along a piece of chalk or a marker, and they come in portable forms.

| Figure 1-9 | CHALKBOARDS EMPHASIZE MAIN POINTS |

On the other hand, these media have disadvantages, including the difficulty of speaking to your audience while you write or draw. If your handwriting is difficult to read, it can detract from your presentation, as can poor spelling. In addition, these media are only effective for writing a few words or short phrases, or making simple drawings.

Using a Flip Chart

Flip charts can be used in both formal and informal settings. Using a flip chart with previously prepared pictures and visuals allows you to highlight the main points of your presentation, and present information in an appropriate sequence. Flip charts work best when used in a small, well-lighted room.

| Figure 1-10 | FLIP CHARTS SHOW SEQUENCE |

The disadvantages of flip charts are that they are too small to be seen in large rooms or by large audiences, they require significant advance preparation, and they are cumbersome.

Using Posters

Posters or written summaries of your presentation that can be displayed on stationary blackboards or attached to the walls of a room are effective for letting audiences refer to your presentation before or after the event. Posters are especially prevalent at academic or professional conferences, and presenters often stand by their posters to answer questions from the audience.

| Figure 1-11 | POSTERS PROVIDE VISUAL SUMMARIES |

Because posters usually contain professional lettering, as well as technical graphics and illustrations, they can't be easily revised, and they do require advance preparation.

Using Black-and-White or Color Overheads

Overheads are used a lot so required equipment is usually accessible. Creating overheads can be as simple as copying your presentation notes onto overhead transparencies. Overheads do require some advance preparation, however, or they look amateurish or uninteresting. In addition, overheads are ineffective if the lettering is too small or too dense.

| Figure 1-12 | OVERHEADS FOCUS ATTENTION |

Overheads allow for flexibility in your presentation as they can quickly be reordered or adjusted, as necessary. You can also draw on overheads using a transparency marker during your presentation.

Using Handouts

Handouts give your listeners something to take with them following your presentation, such as a summary of key points or numerical data. Handouts can assist your listeners in understanding difficult concepts, and can also alleviate the difficulties of taking notes.

Figure 1-13   **HANDOUTS ALLEVIATE NOTE TAKING**

Although handouts are helpful, they require advance preparation to look professional. Also, be careful that your handouts don't detract from your presentation by enticing your audience to pay more attention to them than your presentation.

Using 35mm Slides

Using 35mm slides requires advance preparation, so you must allow enough time to take pictures, and have them developed into professional-looking slides. Slides are especially good for presentations in a formal setting, in large rooms, or with large audiences. Slides require that you turn the lights down, however, which makes it difficult for you to see your presentation notes, for the audience to take notes, and for some people to stay awake. In addition, using slides forces you to choose between facing your audience and standing at a distance from the slide projector, or standing behind the slide projector and talking to the backs of your audience.

Figure 1-14   **SLIDES HELP LARGE AUDIENCES**

You can increase the effectiveness of your slide presentation by using a hand-held remote to advance your slides, and a laser pointer to draw attention to important aspects of the slides. Or, you could give the presentation in tandem with someone else—you as the presenter and the other person as the operator of the equipment.

Using Electronic On-Screen Presentations

Electronic on-screen presentations (such as those created with Microsoft PowerPoint, Corel Presentations, or some other presentation software package) allow you to create professional-looking presentations with a consistent visual design. They also enable you to incorporate other media into your presentations, such as photographs, sound, animation, and video clips. Electronic on-screen presentations are also easy to update or revise on the spot, and can easily be converted into other media, such as overheads, posters, or 35mm slides.

Figure 1-15	INCORPORATE OTHER MEDIA

Electronic on-screen presentations require special equipment such as a computer projection system which may not always be available. And, sometimes you must present your computer presentation in a darkened room, making it difficult for you to see your notes and for your listeners to take notes. You can reduce the difficulty by asking someone else to operate the computer equipment for you.

In addition, electronic on-screen presentations require advance preparation and set up to ensure compatibility of the computer, the projection system, and the disk containing your presentation files. Moreover, many presenters create on-screen presentations that are too elaborate, rather than simple and straightforward.

REFERENCE WINDOW | **RW**

Strengths and Weaknesses of Presentation Media

Type of Medium	Strengths	Weaknesses	Audience Size	Advance Preparation	Formality
Chalkboard Whiteboard Notepad	Enables audience input; good for summarizing; adaptable	Must write and talk simultaneously; requires good handwriting and spelling	Small	None required	Informal
Flip chart	Can highlight main points and sequence information	Too small to be seen in large room; cumbersome	Small	Required	Formal and Informal
Posters	Can be referred to following your presentation; good for displaying other materials	Can't be easily revised; needs explanation	Medium, Large	Required	Formal and Informal
Overheads	Equipment readily available; adaptable; can draw on	Often boring, uninteresting, or ineffective	Medium, Large	Required	Formal and Informal
Handouts	Alleviates taking notes; can be referred to later	Can distract from your presentation	Small, Medium, Large	Required	Formal and Informal
35mm slides	Good for formal presentations in large rooms	Difficult to see your notes and to advance slides; require special equipment	Large	Extensive preparation required	Formal
Electronic on-screen slides	Incorporates media; good for formal presentations in large rooms	May be too elaborate or distracting; require special equipment	Small, Large	Extensive preparation required	Formal

Since every medium has its disadvantages, you might want to use more than one medium in your presentation. At the college you'll give your presentation in a room that isn't equipped with a computer projection system, but does have a large chalkboard and overhead projector. So you might want to create a poster displaying photographs of YES! activities and participants, show an overhead transparency explaining how the partnership between YES! and the university would work, and prepare a handout containing information on YES! service projects.

No matter what media you use, your goal should be to keep your presentation simple and to adapt it to the purpose, audience, and situation of each unique situation.

Figure 1.16 provides a basic worksheet for helping you assess the situation and media for this and other presentations.

Figure 1-16 ○ SITUATION ASSESSMENT WORKSHEET

Situation and Media Assessment
Worksheet

How much time will you have for your presentation and the setup? _____

How large will your audience be? _____

How formal will the setting be? _____

What will the room be like and how will it be arranged? _____

What equipment will be available for your presentation? Check all that apply.
☐ Chalkboard
☐ Whiteboard
☐ Notepad and easel
☐ Stationary posterboard
☐ Overhead projector
☐ Slide projector
☐ Computer projection system

What other aspects must you consider for your presentation?
Temperature _____
Lighting _____
Noise and distractions _____
Other _____

Who will assist you with the equipment and other situational aspects?
Friend or colleague _____
Media or custodial staff _____
Other _____

How will you introduce yourself and your qualifications?
_____
_____
_____

What media will be appropriate for your presentation? Check appropriate media and explain.
☐ Chalkboard _____
☐ Whiteboard _____
☐ Notepad and easel _____
☐ Flip chart _____
☐ Poster _____
☐ Black-and-white or color overheads _____
☐ Handouts _____
☐ 35mm slides _____
☐ Computer Projected visuals, such as PowerPoint slides _____

Session 1.1 QUICK CHECK

1. Define and give examples for the following types of presentations:
   a. informative presentation
   b. persuasive presentation
   c. demonstration or training session

2. In two or three sentences, describe how knowing the education level of an audience would affect a presentation on trademarks and copyright laws.

3. List at least two important questions you should ask as part of assessing the presentation situation.

4. Consider the following presentations. In each instance list two media that would be effective for that presentation, and explain why you think those media would be effective. Then list two media that would be ineffective for that presentation and explain why.
   a. a presentation at the local hardware store to eight to 10 homeowners on how to successfully remodel a kitchen
   b. a presentation at a hotel ballroom to 40 to 50 convention planners on why they should hold their next convention in Colorado Springs
   c. a presentation to two or three administrative staff at a local business on how to conduct a successful Web conference

5. List two media that are useful for recording comments from the audience.

6. If you want to use sound and animation in your presentation, which medium should you use?

SESSION 1.2

In this session, you'll learn how to focus your presentation, and develop an effective introduction, body, and conclusion for that presentation.

Focusing Your Presentation

Once you determine your purpose, analyze your audience's needs and expectations, and assess the particular situation in which you'll give your presentation, you need to plan the content of your presentation. You should begin by identifying the major points or main ideas that are directly relevant to your listeners' needs and interests, and then focus on those.

One of the biggest problems every presenter faces is how to make the topic manageable. Your tendency will be to want to include every aspect of a topic, but trying to cover every facet usually means that you'll give your audience irrelevant information and lose their interest. Focusing on one aspect of a topic is like bringing a picture into focus with your camera—it clarifies your subject and allows you to emphasize interesting details. Failing to focus, in presentations as in photography, always brings disappointment to you and your audience.

How you focus your topic will depend upon the purpose, audience, and situation for your presentation. Remember, the narrower the topic, the more specific and interesting the information will be. Strategies for limiting your presentation topic are the same as those you would use to limit the scope of any written document—focus on a particular time or chronology, geography or region, category, component or element, segment or portion of a procedure, or point of view.

- ■ Time or chronology: Limiting a topic by time means you focus on a few years, rather than trying to cover the entire history of a topic. Unfocused: The history of Egypt from 640 to 2000. Focused: The history of Egypt during the Nasser years (1952–1970).

- ■ Geography or region: Limiting a topic by geography or region means you look at a topic as it relates to a specific location. Unfocused: Fly fishing. Focused: Fly fishing in western Colorado.

- ■ Category or classification: Limiting a topic by category means you focus on one member of a group or on a limited function. Unfocused: Thermometers. Focused: Using bimetallic-coil thermometers to control bacteria in restaurant-prepared foods.

- ■ Component or element: Limiting a topic by component or element means you focus on one small aspect or part of an organization or problem. Unfocused: Business trends. Focused: Blending accounting practices and legal services, a converging trend in large businesses.

- ■ Segment or portion: Limiting a topic by segment or portion means you focus on one part of a process or procedure. Unfocused: Designing, manufacturing, characterizing, handling, storing, packaging, and transporting of optical filters. Focused: Acceptance testing of optical filters.

- ■ Point of view: Limiting a topic by point of view means you look at a topic from the perspective of a single group. Unfocused: Employee benefits. Focused: How employers can retain their employees by providing child-care assistance and other nontraditional benefits.

REFERENCE WINDOW   RW

Ways to Limit Your Topic
- Time or chronology
- Geography or region
- Category or classification
- Component or element
- Segment or portion of a process or procedure
- Point of view or perspective

In your presentation about YES! at Rocky Mountain State College, you'll need to limit your topic. You decide to discuss only current programs needing volunteers, not past or future programs. You'll also limit your presentation to service opportunities in the Colorado Springs area, and not include opportunities at the YES! satellite programs throughout the state. In addition, you'll only present information on volunteer programs, not fundraising, budgeting, or legal functions. Further, you'll only discuss how student volunteers assist with recreation therapy, not physical therapy. Finally, you'll approach your topic from a student volunteer's perspective.

Identifying Your Main Ideas

As you identify your main ideas, you should phrase them as conclusions you want your audience to draw from your presentation. This helps you to continue to design your presentation with the listener in mind.

Your main ideas for your presentation about YES! at Rocky Mountain State College include:

1. University students and their communities benefit when students volunteer with nonprofit organizations such as YES!.

2. Students learn as they participate in service that meets a community need.

3. Students can apply what they learn in the classroom to help solve many social and economic problems in the community.

4. A formal partnership between YES! and the university would assist students in obtaining course credit for their service with nonprofit organizations.

You're now prepared to consider the content and organization of your presentation. In the sections that follow, you'll formulate the general organization of your presentation.

Organizing Your Presentation

Once you've finished planning your presentation, you'll need to assemble the contents of your presentation, and organize your ideas in a logical manner. There are many different ways to organize or arrange your presentation, depending upon your purpose, the needs of your audience, and a particular speaking situation. In general, all good presentations start with an effective introduction, continue with a well-organized body, and end with a strong conclusion.

The introduction of a presentation enables you to gain your listeners' attention, establish a relationship with your audience, and preview your main ideas. The body of your presentation is where you'll present pertinent information, solid evidence, and important details. The conclusion allows you to restate your main points, suggest appropriate actions, and recommend further resources.

REFERENCE   WINDOW   **RW**

<u>General Organization of Presentations</u>

- ■ Introduction
  - Gains and keeps attention of audience
  - Creates a favorable impression
  - Establishes your credibility
  - Provides overview of presentation
- ■ Body
  - Follows main points of presentation
  - Provides evidence and support for main points
  - Presents research in adequate detail
  - Shows relevance of data
- ■ Conclusion
  - Restates main points of presentation
  - Suggests appropriate action
  - Recommends ways of finding additional data

| Figure 1-17 | INTRODUCTION, BODY, AND CONCLUSION |

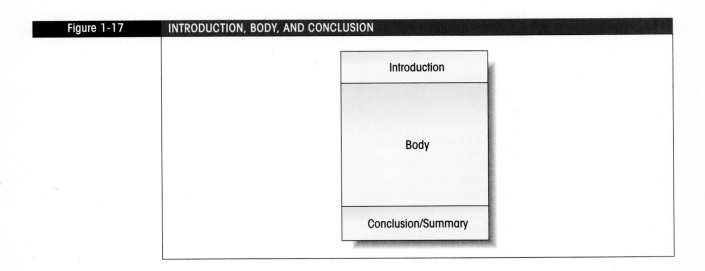

In the next section, you'll learn how to develop the introduction to your presentation.

Developing **an Introduction**

Your introduction is the most important part of your entire presentation because it provides your listeners' first impression of you and your presentation, and sets the tone for the rest of your presentation. An effective introduction enables you to gain your listeners' attention, establish a rapport with your audience, and provide your listeners with an organizational overview or preview of your presentation.

Gaining Your Audience's Attention

Your first task in giving an effective presentation is to gain and keep your audience's attention. Even if your audience is interested in your topic, they can be easily distracted, so it's important to create an effective introduction that will immediately grab their attention.

Here are some ways to gain your audience's attention:

- Anecdotes, stories, or personal experiences
- Surprising statistics or relevant data
- A quotation, familiar phrase, or definition
- Rhetorical questions or unresolved issues and problems
- Comments about the audience or occasion
- Audience participation
- Statement of your topic

Using Anecdotes

Think back to a presentation you attended recently. What do you remember most about it? Isn't it a story or experience that sticks out in your mind? Anecdotes help you to gain your listeners' attention because they draw the listener into your topic and make the topic more personal. Sharing a personal experience helps your audience relate to you as a real person and makes your topic more relevant.

You could begin your presentation at Rocky Mountain State College by relating your personal experience in meeting Chad, a handicapped youth who you helped:

"During my junior year at Rocky Mountain State College, I volunteered to help out at a Sports Camp sponsored by a local nonprofit organization called YES! At the Sports Camp, I met Chad, a 14-year-old who suffers from cerebral palsy. Chad didn't have a lot of friends and spent his time after school alone, playing computer games. During camp, I helped Chad learn to play basketball. Now he spends some of his time after school playing basketball with other kids he met at camp. I'm glad I could help Chad and other kids become more confident and make new friends. But I also benefited. My Recreation Management major now has new meaning. I see how the things I learn in class can be applied in the real world to help kids like Chad."

Using Statistics and Data

Interesting statistics and data relating to the needs of your audience can increase the listeners' interest in knowing more about your topic. Make sure, however, that the statistics and data you use are current, accurate, and easily understood.

In your presentation at Rocky Mountain State College you could refer to interesting and related data:

"Last year, Coloradoans showed their commitment to solving some of our community's problems by donating $827,000 to more than 85 nonprofit organizations in the state. But money isn't the only donation these nonprofits need. Many of them would benefit greatly from a generous donation of your time."

Using Quotations, Familiar Phrases, and Definitions

Short quotes, familiar phrases, or definitions can effectively gain your audience's attention because they lead into the rest of your talk. You could use the following quotation to introduce your presentation at Rocky Mountain State College:

"'A man of words and not of deeds is like a garden full of weeds.' That simple adage could describe our students who currently can't take advantage of opportunities for experiential learning, because Rocky Mountain State College has no academic internship programs or partnerships with local service organizations."

Using Questions

Asking questions to introduce your topic can be effective if the questions are thought-provoking and the issues are important. Rhetorical questions—questions you don't expect the audience to answer—are especially effective. You should exercise caution, however, and not use too many questions. You should also be aware that someone in the audience might call out humorous or otherwise unwanted answers to your questions, detracting from the effectiveness of your introduction, and putting you in an awkward position.

Some examples of rhetorical questions you could use in your presentation at Rocky Mountain State College include:

"Why have colleges and universities across the country begun to establish partnerships with local nonprofit organizations? [Pause] What are the benefits of volunteerism for college students? [Pause] What can we as student leaders do to receive course credit while solving some of the problems in the Colorado Springs community?"

Commenting About the Audience or Occasion

Comments about the audience or occasion enable you to show your enthusiasm about the group you're addressing, as well as about your topic. Remember, however, that your comments should be brief and sincere. Referring to the occasion can be as simple as:

- "I'm happy you've given me an opportunity to express my views about creating a partnership between Rocky Mountain State College and local nonprofit organizations."

- "As you know, Joni de Paula, our student-body president, has invited me to tell you about my experience as an intern with YES!, a local nonprofit organization."

- "As student leaders at Rocky Mountain State College, you're probably interested in the growing movement in higher education to give students college credit for their work in solving local community problems."

Using Audience Participation

Involving your audience in your presentation encourages them to add their ideas to your presentation, rather than to simply sit and listen. Audience participation is especially effective in small group settings or situations where you're attempting to find new ways to approach ideas. Audience participation can also consist of asking for volunteers from the audience to help with your demonstration, or asking audience members to give tentative answers to an informal quiz or questionnaire, and then adjusting your presentation to accommodate their responses.

| Figure 1-18 | AUDIENCES REMEMBER PARTICIPATION |

In your presentation at Rocky Mountain State College, you might ask a few members of the audience to express their feelings about their volunteer efforts in the past.

Stating Your Purpose Statement

Simply stating your purpose statement works well as an introduction if your audience is already interested in your topic, or your time is limited. Most audiences, however, will appreciate a more creative approach than simply stating, "I'm going to persuade you to support a partnership between Rocky Mountain State University and YES!, a local nonprofit organization." Instead you might say something like, "My purpose is to discuss a situation that affects almost every student at Rocky Mountain State University."

Because you'll be giving many presentations throughout your career, you'll want to be on the lookout for ideas for effective introductions. You might want to keep a presentations file for collecting interesting stories and quotations that you can use in preparing future presentations.

REFERENCE WINDOW   **RW**

Ways to Gain Your Audience's Attention

Method for Gaining Attention	Strength of Method
Anecdote or personal experience	Helps audience relate to you as a real person
Surprising statistic or relevant data	Increases audience interest in topic
Quotation, familiar phrase or definition	Leads in well to remainder of presentation
Rhetorical question or issue	Gets audience thinking about topic
Comment about the audience or occasion	Enables you to show your enthusiasm
Audience participation	Encourages audience to add their own ideas
Statement of the topic	Works well if audience is already interested

Establishing a Rapport with Your Audience

The methods you use to gain your audience's attention will establish how the audience responds to you and to your presentation. It's important, then, that whatever you do in your introduction creates a favorable impression with your audience, and helps you establish credibility.

If your audience is unfamiliar with you or no one formally introduces you, you should introduce yourself and provide your credentials to establish a rapport with your audience. Be careful not to spend much time on this, however, or to distance yourself from your audience by over-emphasizing your accomplishments.

In your presentation at Rocky Mountain State College, you might start out by simply saying, "Hi. I'm_____, a Senior at RMSC and a Recreation Management major."

Providing an Overview of Your Presentation

One of the most important aspects of an introduction is to provide your audience with an overview of your presentation. Research indicates that overviews, sometimes called advance organizers, prepare your audience for each point that will follow, and provide them with a structure for plugging in your main points. Overviews help your audience understand and remember your presentation because they provide a road map of it.

Overviews should be brief and simple, stating what you plan to do and in what order. After you've given your audience an overview of your presentation, it's important that you follow that same order.

Avoiding Common Mistakes in an Introduction

An inadequate introduction can ruin the rest of your presentation no matter how well you've prepared. So you should allow yourself plenty of time to carefully plan your introductions. In addition, you should consider these guidelines to avoid common mistakes:

- Don't begin by apologizing about any aspect of your presentation, such as how nervous you are, or your lack of preparation. Apologies destroy your credibility and guarantee that your audience will react negatively to what you present.
- Check the accuracy and currency of your stories, examples, and data. Audiences don't appreciate being misled, misinformed, or manipulated.
- Steer clear of anything potentially vulgar, ridiculing, or sexist. You won't be respected or listened to once you offend your audience.
- Don't use gimmicks to begin your presentation, such as making a funny face, singing a song, or ringing a bell. Members of your audience won't know how to respond and will feel uncomfortable.
- Avoid trite, flattering, or phony statements, such as, "Ladies and gentlemen, it is an unfathomable honor to be in your presence." Gaining respect requires treating your audience as your equal.
- Don't coerce people into participating. Always ask for volunteers. Putting reluctant members of your audience on the spot embarrasses everyone.
- Be cautious when using humor. It's difficult to predict how audiences will respond to jokes and other forms of humor; therefore, you should avoid using humor unless you know your audience well.

Once you've introduced your topic, you're ready to develop the major points or body of your presentation.

Developing **the Body of Your Presentation**

To develop the body of your presentation, you'll need to gather information on your topic, determine the organizational approach, add supporting details and other pertinent information, and provide transitions from one point to the next.

Gathering Information

Most of the time, you'll give presentations on topics about which you're knowledgeable and comfortable. Other times, you might have to give presentations on topics that are new to you. In either case, you'll probably need to do research to provide additional information that is effective, pertinent, and up-to-date.

You can find additional materials on your topic by consulting:

- Popular press items from newspapers, radio, TV, and magazines. This information, geared for general audiences, provides surface-level details and personal opinions that may need to be supplemented by additional research.

Figure 1-19	USING NEWSPAPERS AND MAGAZINES

■ Library resources such as books, specialized encyclopedias, academic journals, government publications, and other reference materials. You can access these materials using the library's card catalog, indexes, computer searches, and professional database services.

Figure 1-20	USING INFORMATION IN LIBRARIES

■ Corporate documents and office correspondence. Since using these materials might violate your company's nondisclosure policy, you might need to obtain your company's permission, or get legal clearance.

Figure 1-21	USING CORPORATE DOCUMENTS

■ Experts and authorities in the field, or other members of your organization. Talking to others who are knowledgeable about your topic will give you additional insight.

Figure 1-22	TALKING TO EXPERTS AND AUTHORITIES

■ Interviews, surveys, and observations. If you do your own interviews, surveys, and observations, be prepared with a list of specific questions, and always be respectful of other people's time.

| Figure 1-23 | INTERVIEWING AND SURVEYING |

■ Internet sources. The Web has become an excellent place to find information on any topic. Be sure, however, to evaluate the credibility of anything you obtain from these sources.

| Figure 1-24 | USING THE INTERNET |

For your presentation at Rocky Mountain State College, you located the following additional information: an article from the *Colorado Springs Daily Scribe* entitled, "YES! Helps Children Meet Their Challenges;" a book from the RMSC library entitled, *A Guidebook for Providing Opportunities for Experiential Education in Higher Education*; the YES! organization's latest annual report; an informal survey of 25 current interns showing their attitudes toward establishing a partnership between YES! and RMSC; and printouts of the YES! Web page describing the organization's funding sources and current activities.

After you fully research your topic, you're ready to organize the information in an understandable and logical manner so that your listeners can easily follow your ideas.

Organizing Your Information

You should choose an organizational approach for your information based upon the purpose, audience, and situation of each specific presentation. Sometimes your company or supervisor might ask you to follow a particular pattern or template in giving your presentations. Other times you might be able to choose your own organizational approach. Some common approach options include: inductive, deductive, chronological, spatial, and problem-solution organizational patterns.

Organizing Information Inductively

Organizing information inductively means you begin with the individual facts and save your conclusions until the end of your presentation. Inductively organized presentations usually are more difficult to follow because the most important information may come at the end of a presentation. Inductive organization can be useful, however, when your purpose is to persuade your audience to follow an unusual plan of action, or you feel your audience might resist your conclusions.

| Figure 1-25 | INDUCTIVE ORGANIZATION |

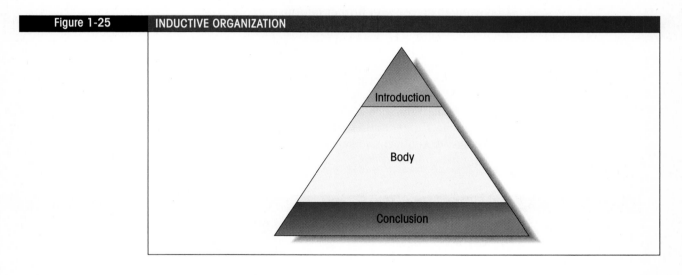

If you thought student leaders at Rocky Mountain State College would resist your recommendation (that $600,000 from student fees be allocated to the operating budget of a new Student Community Involvement Center), you would probably want to first present your reasons for making that recommendation.

Organizing Information Deductively

Organizing information deductively means you present your conclusions or solutions first, and then explain the information that led you to reach your conclusions. Deductive organization is the most common pattern used in business because it presents the most important or bottom-line information first.

Figure 1-26	DEDUCTIVE ORGANIZATION

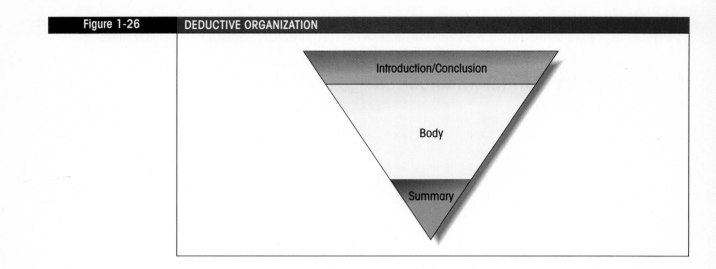

Deductive organization works well for informative presentations because it allows your audience to know your recommendations at the beginning of the presentation when their attention level is highest. Organizing your presentation at Rocky Mountain State College in a deductive manner would mean that you would begin by stating your opinion that student leaders should support an official partnership between the university and YES!, and then supporting that view with further information.

Organizing Information Chronologically

When you organize information chronologically, you organize things according to a time sequence. Chronological organization works best when you must present information in a step-by-step fashion, such as demonstrating a procedure, or training someone to use a piece of equipment. Failing to present sequential information in the proper order (such as how to bake a cake, or conduct a soil analysis) can leave your listeners confused, and might result in wasting time and resources.

Figure 1-27	CHRONOLOGICAL ORGANIZATION

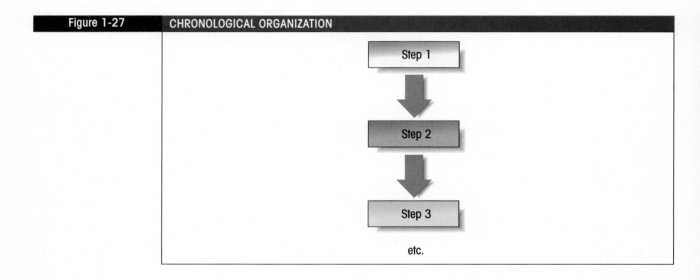

If you were explaining to administrators how to answer a Request for Proposal (RFP) to obtain government funding for YES! activities, you would need to explain how to complete the process in a specified sequence.

Organizing Information Spatially

Spatial organization is used to provide a logical and effective order for describing the physical layout of an item or system.

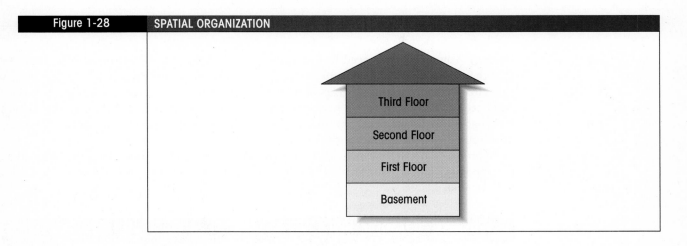

| Figure 1-28 | SPATIAL ORGANIZATION |

If you were describing the blueprints or plans for a new building for YES!, you would begin by describing all the rooms on the bottom floor, then proceed to the next floor and describe all the rooms on that floor, and so on.

Organizing Information by Problem and Solutions

Using the problem-solution method of organization consists of presenting a problem, outlining various solutions to the problem, and then explaining the solution you recommend. Problem-solution presentations work best when your purpose is to recommend a specific action or solution over several alternative actions or solutions.

REFERENCE WINDOW   RW

Ways to Organize Your Presentation

Organizational Pattern	Explanation of Pattern	Type of Presentation
Deductive	Present conclusions or solutions first	Informative presentations
Inductive	Present conclusions or solutions last	Persuasive presentations
Chronological	Order by time sequence	Demonstrations and training
Spatial	Order by space or position	Physical layouts
Problem/Solution	Present problem and various solutions, then recommend solution	Persuasive presentations

Supporting **Your Main Points**

In every presentation, it's important to keep the information simple and relevant. Research has shown that our short-term memory limits what we can recall to a maximum of seven chunks of information, and that we remember specific, concrete details long after we remember generalities or unrelated pieces of information.

You should, therefore, support the main points of your presentation with evidence in the form of specific reasons, explanations, examples, data, or agreement of experts. In addition, you should try to intersperse difficult concepts with easier-to-understand material, and try to move from what your audience already understands to new information.

Providing Transitions

In any presentation, you need to provide organizational signposts or transitions that indicate the organization and structure of your presentation. Transitions enable your listeners to realize that you're shifting gears or moving to a new topic. Effective transitions help your audience mentally summarize what you have discussed previously and prepare themselves for what you'll discuss next. Transitions also enable you to pause briefly to check your notes or to reestablish eye contact with your audience.

Appropriate transitions include words that indicate you will provide examples, make additional points, compare similar concepts, discuss results, or make recommendations. Transitions may include:

REFERENCE WINDOW	RW
Purpose	**Word or Phrase**
Provide examples	For example, For instance, To illustrate
Make additional points	In addition, Furthermore, Next, Now I will discuss
Establish order	First, Second, Third
Compare	Likewise, In the same manner, Let's consider another
Discuss results	Consequently, Therefore, Thus
Summarize	In brief, To conclude, To move to my last point, Finally
Recommend	I'd like to suggest, What do we do now?

Now that you've developed an effective body for your presentation by supporting your main points with adequate details and creating effective transitions, you're ready to develop a conclusion or summary.

Developing Your Summary or Conclusion

Summaries and conclusions are valuable because they help your listeners remember important information from your presentation and allow you to reemphasize your main points. Your conclusion leaves your audience with a final impression of you and your presentation, so you don't want to leave your conclusion to chance. Plan to spend as much time on the conclusion as you did on your introduction.

The following suggestions will help you create an effective summary or conclusion:

- Use a clear transition to move into your conclusion. This will signal your audience that you're moving from the body of your presentation to the closing statements.
- Recap the key ideas of your presentation. Repeating the main points of your presentation will help your audience remember what you covered.
- Review the relevancy or importance of what you said. Don't introduce new ideas; simply remind your audience why they should care about your topic.
- If appropriate, suggest a clear action step or plan. If your purpose was to persuade your audience to take a specific action, you should use your conclusion to suggest what the audience should do now.

- If possible, suggest where your audience can find additional resources by providing important phone numbers, addresses, e-mail addresses, or Web addresses.

- Relate your conclusion to your introduction. Some experts suggest writing your conclusion at the same time you write your introduction to assure that they both provide the same focus. Whenever you write your conclusion, compare it to your introduction to make sure they are complementary.

- Don't end with an apology or trite statement like "I see my time is up, so I'll quit." When you're finished, say "Thank you," and sit down.

In your presentation at Rocky Mountain State College, you could conclude your presentation by stating, "Now that you've seen how a formal partnership between YES! and the university would work, I'd like to briefly summarize the main points I've made today. First, university students and the communities in which they live both benefit when students volunteer with nonprofit organizations. Second, students become active learners as they apply what they learn in the classroom to help solve community problems. Finally, it's important to establish a formal partnership between these nonprofit organizations and the university so that students can obtain course credit for their work. By allocating $600,000 from student fees toward the operating budget of a new Student Community Involvement Center, you can help students take advantage of opportunities for experiential learning, while helping Chad and the 1300 other young people like him."

Figure 1-29 provides a basic worksheet for helping you determine the focus and organization for this and other presentations.

Figure 1-29	FOCUS AND ORGANIZATION WORKSHEET

Focus and Organization
Worksheet

How will you focus your presentation?
Time or chronology _____
Geography or region _____
Category or classification _____
Component or element _____
Segment or portion _____
Point of view _____

What are your main ideas for your presentation?
_____
_____
_____

How will you gain your audience's attention?
Anecdote, story, or personal experience _____
Statistic or relevant data _____
Quotation, familiar phrase, or definition _____
Rhetorical question, issue, or problem _____
Comment about audience or situation _____
Audience participation _____
Statement of topic _____

How will you establish a rapport with your audience?
_____
_____

Where can you find additional information about your presentation?
Newspapers or magazines _____
Library resources _____
Corporate documents _____
Experts and authorities _____
Interviews and surveys _____
Internet sources _____

How will you organize your information? Check one and then explain it.
☐ Inductively ☐ Deductively ☐ Chronologically ☐ Spatially ☐ Problem/Solution
_____
_____

How will you support your main points?
_____
_____

What transitions will you use?
_____
_____

How will you conclude or summarize your presentation?
_____
_____

In this tutorial, you learned how to plan and organize your presentation based upon the needs of your audience and the presentation situation. In Tutorial 2, you'll learn how to use effective visuals in your presentation, and how to deliver your message with confidence and clarity.

Session 1.2 QUICK CHECK

1. List three methods for focusing your topic.

2. Determine which methods have been used to focus the following topics: (a) Creating E-commerce Solutions for Small Business Owners (b) How to Submit Winning Bids: Obtaining Government Contracts.

3. Why should you phrase the main ideas of your presentation as conclusions you want your audience to draw?

4. What are the three basic parts of every presentation, and what is the purpose of each part?

5. List one advantage for each of the following ways to gain your audience's attention: (a) personal experience (b) statistics or data (c) rhetorical questions.

6. List four places to find additional materials on a topic.

7. What is the difference between organizing your presentation deductively and inductively, and when would you use each of these organizational patterns?

8. Give an example of a transitional phrase you could use to indicate that you're moving to your next main point.

REVIEW ASSIGNMENTS

While you're preparing your presentation to student leaders at Rocky Mountain State College, your supervisor, Kenna McNaughton, decides to have you give three presentations at Rampart High School, also in Colorado Springs.

The first presentation will be a 30-minute, informative presentation on the value of community service. You'll give this presentation, as part of a school assembly, to over 200 students in a large, computer-equipped auditorium with fixed seating.

The second presentation will be a 15-minute, persuasive presentation to teachers on giving credit for service assignments. You'll give this presentation as part of a faculty in-service meeting, to approximately 35 teachers in a faculty lounge with small tables and movable chairs.

The third presentation will be a 50-minute presentation for Senior class officers on how to plan a successful service project. You'll give this presentation as part of a leadership training session, to about six students in a medium-sized classroom with movable desks. Do the following:

1. Complete a Purpose and Outcomes Worksheet for the three types of presentations.

2. Explain differences and similarities between the three groups in terms of the following demographic features: age, gender, and level of education. Then complete an Audience Analysis Worksheet for the three types of presentations.

3. Explain how the settings for these presentations will affect your audience's expectations and the appropriate level of formality. Then complete a Situation and Media Assessment Worksheet for the three types of presentations.

4. Determine appropriate and inappropriate media for each of the three presentations.

5. Give an example of how you could focus the topic for the first presentation by limiting it by geography or region.

6. Give an example of how you could focus the second presentation by limiting it by point of view.

7. Give an example of how you could focus the third presentation by limiting it by category or classification.

8. Prepare an introduction for the first presentation using a story or anecdote. (You may create a fictional anecdote.)

9. Prepare an introduction for the second presentation using rhetorical questions.

10. Prepare an introduction for the third presentation using some kind of audience participation.

11. List two places to find additional information on the topics of each of these presentations.

12. Determine an appropriate organizational pattern for each of the three presentations.

13. Complete a Focus and Organization Worksheet for each of the three presentations.

CASE PROBLEMS

Case 1. American Cancer Society   The American Cancer Society is a well-known nonprofit organization with chapters in nearly every state and county. Working with another member of the class, create a team presentation to inform your classmates about the goals and programs of the American Cancer Society organization in your area. You should be able to get information about the organization by consulting your local United Way organization, or by searching the Internet.

1. Decide on a type of presentation.

2. Complete a Purpose and Outcomes Worksheet.

3. Define your audience according to their general demographic features of age, gender, level of education, and familiarity with your topic.

4. Explain how the demographic characteristics of your audience will affect your presentation. Then complete an Audience Analysis Worksheet.

5. Describe the setting for your presentation and the size of your audience. Then complete a Situation and Media Assessment Worksheet.

6. Select appropriate media for your presentation and explain why they are appropriate. Explain why other media are inappropriate.

7. Show two ways to focus your presentation and limit the scope of your topic.

8. Each of you should select a method for gaining your audience's attention and write an introduction using that method. Discuss the strengths of each method for your particular audience.

9. Create an advance organizer, or overview.

10. Identify at least two sources for information on your topic and consult those sources. Print out at least one page of information that supports the main points of your presentation.

11. Select an appropriate organizational pattern for your presentation. Explain why that pattern is appropriate.

12. Identify four transitional phrases that you'll use.

13. Write a summary for your presentation recapping the key ideas.

14. Complete a Focus and Organization Worksheet.

Case 2. Safelee Home Security Products Sudhir Raguskus is director of marketing for Safelee Home Security Products. The company currently markets a new line of home security systems that includes hardware (alarms, automated lighting, and deadbolt locks) and monitoring services. Sudhir asks you to help prepare presentations for his company. Do the following:

1. Complete a Purpose and Outcomes Worksheet for each of these audiences: (a) sales personnel (b) potential clients (c) public safety officials who will be notified by Safelee in cases of emergency

2. Explain the differences and similarities between the above three groups in terms of the following demographic features: age, level of education, and familiarity with the subject. Complete an Audience Analysis Worksheet for each of the three presentations.

3. Explain the likely settings for these presentations and how these will affect your audience's expectations and dictate the appropriate level of formality.

4. Determine appropriate and inappropriate media for each of the three presentations. Complete a Situation and Media Assessment Worksheet for each of the three-presentations.

5. Give an example of how to focus or limit each presentation.

6. Identify three main ideas of your presentation to potential clients.

7. Prepare an appropriate introduction for each presentation. (Some of your introductory information may be fictional.)

8. Determine how to establish a rapport with public safety officials.

9. List two places to find additional information on the topics of each of these presentations.

10. Determine an appropriate organizational pattern for each of the three presentations.

11. Write an effective conclusion for each of the three presentations.

12. Complete a Focus and Organization Worksheet for each of the three presentations.

Case 3. EVENTix EVENTix owns and operates transactional kiosks that sell mall gift certificates and event/entertainment tickets. Konda Cameron, marketing director for EVENTix, asks you to prepare several presentations about EVENTix. Do the following:

1. Think of the most recent event (such as a concert, sports event, or movie) that you attended. Complete a Purpose and Outcomes Worksheet for a presentation to participants of the event, trying to convince them that they should purchase future events tickets from EVENTix.

2. Complete a Purpose and Outcomes Worksheet for a presentation to participants of the event, explaining how to obtain tickets from an EVENTix kiosk.

3. Complete a Purpose and Outcomes Worksheet for a presentation to participants of the event, informing them of other events for which EVENTix sells tickets.

4. Konda asks you to present information about EVENTix's gift certificate programs at a retailers convention. You'll give your 15-minute presentation in the ballroom of a hotel to over 300 conference attendees. Describe how your presentation will be influenced by this situation. Complete an Audience Analysis Worksheet.

5. Determine appropriate media for the convention presentation if no on-screen technology is available.

6. Complete a Situation and Media Assessment Worksheet.

7. Give an example of how to focus your topic for this particular audience.

8. Create an appropriate attention-getting introduction for your presentation. Explain why other attention getters might be inappropriate.

9. Determine an appropriate organizational pattern.

10. Complete a Focus and Organization Worksheet.

Case 4. Analyzing an Oral Presentation Attend or read a presentation, lecture, or speech and, if possible, obtain a transcript of the presentation. Make copies of your notes or the complete transcript of the presentation for your teacher. Do the following:

1. Complete a Purpose and Outcomes Worksheet.

2. Describe the audience for the presentation, including any general demographics that you can determine. Complete an Audience Analysis Worksheet.

3. Describe where the presentation was given, including the setting and the number of people attending the presentation.

4. Describe the media the speaker used for the presentation. Explain whether or not you feel the media were appropriate, and whether other media would have been more effective. (For instance, if overheads were used, would it have been more effective to use an online electronic presentation?) Complete a Situation and Media Assessment Worksheet.

5. Identify how the speaker established a rapport with the audience.

6. Describe any mistakes the speaker may have made in apologizing to the audience, or failing to consider the needs of the audience. How could these mistakes have been prevented?

7. Determine the structure of the presentation. If you have a written copy of the presentation, mark the introduction, body, and conclusion on the copy.

8. Describe how the speaker gained the audience's attention.

9. Identify whether the speaker provided an overview, or preview, of the presentation. If you have a written copy of the presentation, underline any overviews or previews.

10. Identify the major points in the presentation. If you have a written copy of the presentation, underline the details the presenter used to support these major points.

11. Identify the organizational pattern used in the presentation. Explain whether or not you think the organizational pattern was effective, or if another organizational pattern might have been better.

12. Identify any transitional phrases the speaker used.

13. Describe how the speaker ended the presentation. Explain whether or not you felt the ending was effective.

14. Complete a Focus and Organization Worksheet.

15. Interview a professional in your field and ask about the types of presentations he or she gives. Organize these into the types of presentations given above. Explain your findings.

QUICK | CHECK ANSWERS

Session 1.1

1. (a) explains background information, knowledge, and details about a topic; academic and professional conference presentations, briefings, reviews, reports, meetings, luncheon or dinner speeches, informal symposia. (b) convinces audience to feel or act a certain way; recommendations, sales, action plans, strategy sessions, motivational speeches. (c) demonstrations: show how something works; product and services overviews, computer software demonstrations. Training sessions: give hands-on practice and feedback on performance; employee orientation, seminars, workshops, classes, courses.

2. Audiences with specialized education, such as lawyers, would expect you to use specialized terms; audiences with less education would need more explanations and definitions.

3. How much time will I have? Will I be speaking alone? How large of an audience? How formal or informal of a setting? What will the room be like? How will the room be arranged? What equipment will be available? How much time will I have to set up? What other aspects must I consider? Will I need to introduce myself?

4. (a) effective: flip chart, poster, handout; they work with small informal groups and don't require additional equipment. Ineffective: 35mm slides and computer-projected visuals; they're better for larger, more formal presentations. (b) effective: posters, black-and-white or color overheads, 35mm slides, computer-projected visuals; they're better for large groups where visuals need to be enlarged, and for formal presentations. (c) chalkboard, whiteboard, notepad, handout; they're best for small groups where audience involvement is important.

5. chalkboard, whiteboard, notepad

6. computer-projected slides

Session 1.2

1. by time or chronology, geography or region, category or classification, component or element, segment or portion, point of view.

2. (a) category, component, point of view (b) category, component, segment

3. True

4. introduction (to gain and keep attention, create favorable impression, establish credibility, present overview), body (provide evidence and support for main points, present research, show relevance), conclusion (restate main points, suggest action, recommend additional sources)

5. (a) draw audience into the topic, makes topic more personal and relevant, helps audience relate to you as a person (b) increase interest in topic (c) address thought-provoking and important issues

6. popular press, library resources, corporate documents, experts, interviews, surveys, observations, Internet

7. deductive: presents conclusions first and reasoning second; informative presentations. inductive: presents reasons first, conclusions last; persuasive presentations, or when audience will resist conclusions

8. in addition, furthermore, next, now I will discuss

OBJECTIVES

In this tutorial you will:

- Select and create appropriate and effective visuals

- Present your visuals

- Choose an appropriate delivery method

- Overcome your nervousness and control your speaking anxiety

- Improve your delivery

- Analyze your non-verbal communication

- Set up for your presentation

GIVING YOUR PRESENTATION

Presentation to the Student Senate at Rocky Mountain State College

CASE

Giving Your Presentation at Rocky Mountain State College

Joni de Paula, student body president at Rocky Mountain State College (RMSC), invites you to talk about your experiences as a YES! intern with members of the RMSC Student Senate as part of their deliberations over a proposed partnership with local nonprofit organizations. You planned and organized your presentation; now you'll prepare to give it.

In this tutorial, you'll learn the benefits of using visuals in your presentations, and how to select and create appropriate visuals. You'll also choose an appropriate method for delivering your presentation, and learn ways to improve your delivery. Finally, you'll learn how to set up for your presentation.

SESSION 2.1

In this session you'll learn the skills for effectively using visuals in your presentation: how visuals can benefit your presentation; how to select visuals that are appropriate for your purpose, audience, and situation; and how to effectively present those visuals.

Understanding the Benefits of Using Visuals in Your Presentation

It's much more difficult for people to understand and remember what they hear versus what they see. You can help your listeners comprehend and retain the ideas from your presentation by supplementing your presentation with effective visual aids. The old adage, "A picture is worth a thousand words" especially applies to presentations because listeners understand ideas faster when they can see and hear what you're talking about. Using visuals such as tables, charts, and graphs, to supplement your presentation:

- increases your audience's understanding. Visuals are especially helpful in explaining a difficult concept, displaying data, and illustrating the steps in a process.

- helps listeners remember information. Audiences will remember information longer when you use visuals to highlight or exemplify your main points, review your conclusions, and explain your recommendations.

- highlights your organization. Visuals can serve the same purpose as headings in a printed manuscript by allowing your audience to see how all the parts of your presentation fit together. Visuals can also help you preview and review main points, and differentiate between the main points and the sub-points.

- adds credibility to your presentation. Speakers who use visuals in their presentation are judged by their audiences as more professional and better prepared, as well as more interesting.

- stimulates and maintains your listeners' attention. It's much more interesting to see how something functions, rather than just hear about it. Giving your listeners somewhere to focus their attention keeps them from being distracted or bored.

- varies the pace of your presentation. Visuals enable you to provide sensory variety in your presentation, and keep your presentation from becoming monotonous.

- keeps you on track. Visuals not only benefit your audience, but also help you by providing a means for remembering what you want to say, and for staying on track.

In your presentation at Rocky Mountain State College, if you want to present information showing how the number of students involved in internships has dramatically increased in the last few years, you could simply read a summary of the numbers, as shown in Figure 2-1.

Figure 2-1   WRITTEN SUMMARY

Internship Data Presented in Verbal Format

In the fall of 1989, the number of students at Rocky Mountain State College involved in internships, hit an unprecedented peak at 90. Then for the next three years, it fell almost steadily, dropping to 87 in 1990, 76 in 1991, 66 in 1992, and 43 in 1993. There was slight upsurge in 1994 to 50, then another little drop in 1995 to 42. Then in 1996, the tide seemed to turn, as the number of interns began to go up, first to 52, then to 60 in 1997. In the four years from 1998 to 2002, the number of students opting for an internship more than doubled, as the number grew from 66 to 86 in 1998 and 1999. In 2000, the number of interns stood at 95, increasing to 113 in 2001 and 120 in 2002.

But reading a long series of numbers would be difficult for your audience to understand, and it would be boring. By using visuals, you can present the same data in a format that's easier to understand, and more interesting. You can present the data in tabular format, as shown in Figure 2-2.

Figure 2-2   TABULAR SUMMARY

Internship Data Presented in Visual Format

Year	Number of interns
1989	90
1990	87
1991	76
1992	66
1993	43
1994	50
1995	42
1996	52
1997	60
1998	66
1999	86
2000	95
2001	113
2002	120

Or, you might want to create a graph instead, as shown in Figure 2-3.

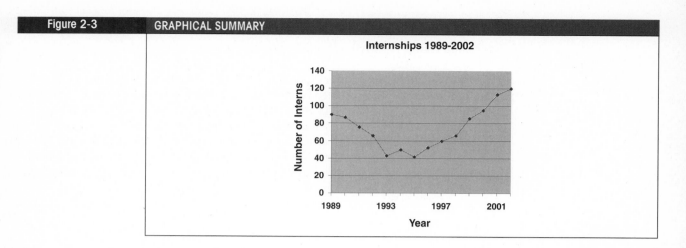

Figure 2-3   GRAPHICAL SUMMARY

Using visuals improves the quality of your presentation, and enables your audience to better understand your presentation. Visuals add information, clarification, emphasis, variety, and even pizzazz to your presentation.

You can choose from many types of visuals for your presentations: tables (text and numerical), graphs (bar and line), charts (pie, organizational, flow), and illustrations (drawings and diagrams, maps, and photographs). In the past, creating visuals was expensive, but the recent development of inexpensive computer software allows you to quickly and inexpensively create tables and graphs, scan photographs, resize drawings, and download visuals from the Internet for your presentation.

To effectively use visuals in your presentations, you'll need to ask yourself which visuals are best for your particular purpose, audience, and situation. You should also ask yourself which visuals you can create effectively.

REFERENCE WINDOW   RW

Selecting Appropriate Visuals
- Which visuals are suitable for my purpose and desired outcomes?
- Which visuals would my audience understand?
- Which visuals work best for the situation in which I'll give my presentation?
- Which visuals can I create effectively?

Answering these questions to the best of your ability will increase the chances that your visuals will be effective.

Selecting Appropriate Visuals for Your Purpose

The following sections provide suggestions to help you select appropriate visuals—tables, graphs, charts, or illustrations—for your particular purpose.

Using Tables

Tables organize words and numerical data in horizontal rows and vertical columns. Tables are especially useful in informative presentations where your purpose is to provide your audience with specific information in a systematic and economical manner. Tables are also effective in:

- making facts and details accessible
- organizing data by categories
- summarizing results and recommendations
- comparing sets of data
- facilitating decisions

In your presentation at RMSC, you might want to explain the many benefits students receive as a result of volunteering in their local communities. You could use a table to summarize and emphasize the broad benefits as well as the specific benefits within each main category. See Figure 2-4.

Figure 2-4	TEXTUAL TABLE

Benefits of Academic Volunteerism	
Category	**Specific Benefits**
Develops civic values	Focus on relationships, rather than content Understand other cultures and needs Gain sense of ethical duty
Improves professional development	Develop problem-solving skills Improve rhetorical skills Practice professional skills
Inspires students	Develop personal philosophy Become aware of learning Increase involvement

Or, perhaps you want to show the number of students who completed internships in the past year. You could use a table to make those numbers more accessible to your audience. Using a table allows you to organize the number of interns according to semester, and the student's year in school. See Figure 2-5.

Figure 2-5	NUMERICAL TABLE

Number of Students Completing an Internship During the School Year 2000-2001 (by Semester)				
	Fall	Summer	Winter	Total
Freshman	0	2	2	4
Sophomore	1	6	3	10
Junior	11	13	13	37
Senior	15	14	15	44
Total	27	35	33	95

In both instances, using a table (figures 2-4 and 2-5) allows you to organize the information so that your audience can quickly see and understand your presentation.

Using the Table feature of your word processor, you can create professional-looking tables. Remember to follow these suggestions to make your tables more effective:

- Keep the table simple. Limit the amount of text and numerical data you use. Dense text is difficult to read, and complex numbers are difficult to understand.
- Use a descriptive title and informative headings. Use a title that explains what you're summarizing or comparing, and label rows and columns so your readers know what they're looking at.
- Remove excess horizontal and vertical lines. To simplify your table, use as few vertical and horizontal lines as possible.
- Use shading and emphasis sparingly. Shading and textual features, such as bolding, italics, and underlining, can be distracting. Don't use heavy shading, and keep textual variety to the main headings.
- Align numbers by place value.
- Keep all numbers consistent in value and number of significant digits.

Whether or not you use a table in your presentation will depend on your purpose. Although tables are good for showing exact numbers (such as, how many Juniors completed an internship during fall semester), they're not as good for showing trends (for instance, the increase or decrease over the past five years in the number of internships).

Using Graphs

Graphs show the relationship between two variables along two axes: the independent variable on the horizontal axis, and the dependent variable on the vertical axis. Like tables, graphs can show a lot of information concisely. Graphs are especially useful in informative presentations when you're showing quantities, or in persuasive presentations when you're comparing similar options using factors such as cost. Graphs are also effective for:

- comparing one quantity to another
- showing changes over time
- indicating patterns or trends

Common graphs include bar graphs and line graphs. **Bar graphs** are useful in comparing the value of one item to another over a period of time, or a range of dates or costs. In your presentation at RMSC, suppose you want to show the difference between the number of men and women completing internships with nonprofit agencies over the past 12 years. By using a bar graph, you could easily compare the differences between students. See Figure 2-6.

Figure 2-6	BAR GRAPH

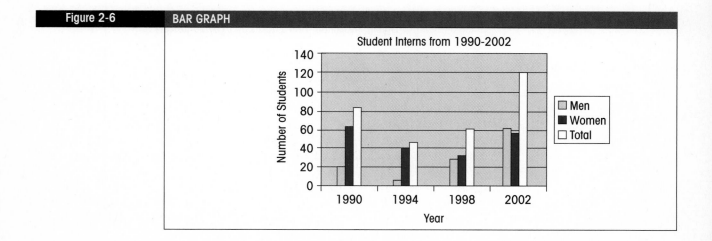

Line graphs are especially effective for illustrating trends. You should use them instead of bar graphs when you have large amounts of information, and exact quantities don't require emphasis. Suppose you want to show the number of youths participating in YES!-sponsored activities during the first six months of each of the last three years (1999-2001). Using a bar chart would require 18 different bars. A more effective way to show the data would be a line graph, as shown in Figure 2-7. Your audience would immediately recognize that, while the number of youth participants has fluctuated in other years, it currently remains constant.

Figure 2-7	LINE GRAPH

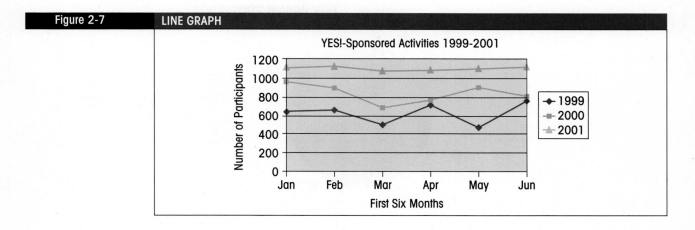

Whether or not you use a graph in your presentation will depend on your purpose. If you choose to use a graph, follow these guidelines:

- Keep graphs simple, clear, and easy to read. Limit the number of comparisons to no more than five.
- Compare values that are noticeably different. Comparing values that are similar means that all the bars will appear identical, and all the lines will overlap.
- Make each bar or line visually distinct. Use a different pattern, shade, or color for each line or bar in a group, and keep bars the same width.
- Label each line and bar. Remember that you're trying to help your listeners understand and use the information.
- Label both axes.

You can create simple bar graphs and line graphs by using the graphing feature of your spreadsheet or database program, or the chart feature of your word-processing or presentations program.

Using Charts

The terms **chart** and graph often are used interchangeably; however, they are distinct. While charts show relationships, they don't use a coordinate system like graphs. Charts are especially helpful in presentations where your goal is to help your listener understand the relationships between the parts and the whole.

Common charts include pie charts, organizational charts, and flowcharts.

Pie charts are best for showing percentages or proportions of the parts that make up a whole. Pie charts allow your listeners to compare the sections to each other, as well as to the whole. Pie charts can be created to display either the percentage relationship or the amount relationship.

Whether or not you use a pie chart in your presentation will depend on your purpose. In your presentation at RMSC, you want to explain how nonprofit organizations, such as YES!, provide assistance to the residents of the Colorado Springs area. You could do that by using a pie chart to show what percent of the agency's budget is allotted to its priority programs, such as self-sufficiency training. See Figure 2-8. Or, you could create the pie chart to show the amounts spent on each type of program.

Figure 2-8	PIE CHART

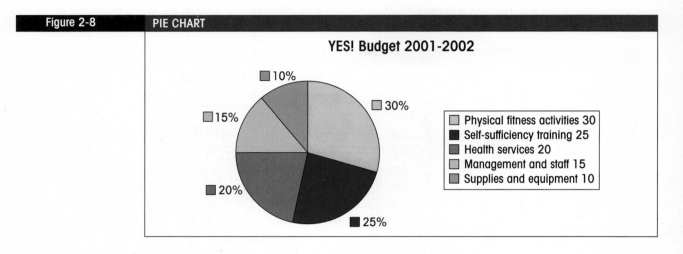

General suggestions for creating effective pie charts include

- Keep slices of the pie relatively large. Comparisons of more than eight sections are difficult to see and differentiate. If necessary, combine several small sections into a section titled, "Other."

- Use a descriptive title for the whole and label each segment. Help your audience understand what you're comparing in terms of the whole, as well as each section of the pie. Keep all labels horizontal so they can be read easily.

- Make sure the parts add up to 100 percent.

- Begin the largest section at the top of the pie. The largest section should begin at the 12 o'clock position. The other sections should get smaller as they move around the pie clockwise, except for the "Other" section, which is usually the last section.

- Use a normal flat pie chart, unless it has fewer than five slices. In other words, you should *not* display the pie chart with 3D perspective, pulled-out pie slices, or in donut format. These effects can detract from seeing the pie as a whole, and can make the chart difficult to read.

You can create simple pie charts by entering your data into a spreadsheet program and then using the graphing feature of that program, or you can use a program such as Microsoft Chart directly in Word, PowerPoint, or other applications software.

Organizational charts show the hierarchical structure of a company or other organization, illustrating the relationship between departments, for example. In your presentation at Rocky Mountain State College, you could show the structure of the YES! organization by creating an organizational chart, as shown in Figure 2-9.

Figure 2-9   ORGANIZATIONAL CHART

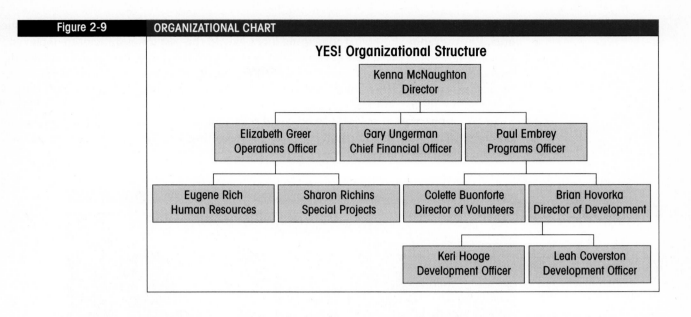

You can create organizational charts using the Organization Chart feature in Microsoft applications. There are also a number of software applications designed specifically for creating charts.

Flowcharts are useful for describing the steps in a procedure, or stages in a decision-making process. Flowcharts are especially effective in demonstrations and training presentations because they can visually supplement verbal instructions, and show the results of alternative decisions. See Figure 2-10.

Figure 2-10   FLOWCHART

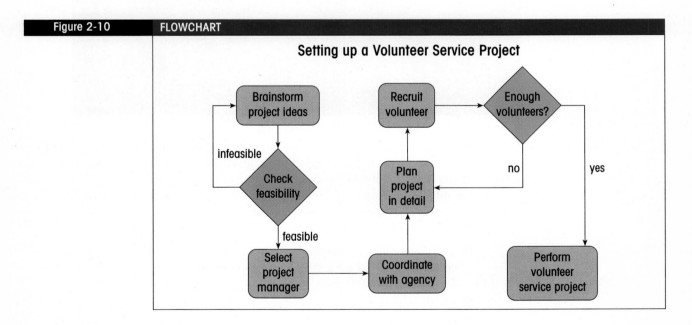

Using Illustrations

Illustrations, including diagrams, drawings, maps, photographs, and clip art, are helpful in showing relationships that aren't numerical. You can use **diagrams** and simple drawings to show how to assemble a piece of equipment, or how the parts of an item or process are related to each other.

Maps are helpful for showing spatial relationships (position and location) in a geographic area. **Photographs** show what something looks like. In the past it was difficult to obtain and use photographs in presentation visuals, but now it is relatively easy because of digital cameras and scanners. Moreover, you can improve the quality of your photographs by removing blemishes, enhancing the colors and contrast, cropping, and making other modifications with photo-editing software.

In your presentation at RMSC, you could scan a picture (or take one with a digital camera) of student interns. You could then use photo-editing software to enhance the picture, enlarge it, and use it on a poster. See Figure 2-11.

Figure 2-11	PHOTOGRAPH

Clip art consists of collections of easy-to-use images that have been bundled with computer programs or purchased separately. Although clip art is readily available, not all clip art images are the same quality. Whenever you use clip art, you should make sure the image is professional-looking and appropriate for your presentation. There are also many Web sites that offer free still and animated clips, as well as sound clips.

General guidelines for using illustrations in your presentations include:

- Use illustrations to supplement your main points. You should use illustrations, especially photographs, in a presentation because they convey meaning, not because they look pretty.

- Make diagrams and drawings accurate. New computer technology enables you to retrieve, edit, and even alter an image. Distorting the image can make it harder for your listeners to recognize and accurately interpret the illustration.

- Provide scale and focus. Crop or trim photographs to emphasize what is important and eliminate unnecessary details.

■ Abide by all copyright laws. Illustrations, including photographs and clip art, retrieved from the Internet are subject to copyright laws. Make sure you understand and abide by copyright laws.

■ Avoid plagiarism. If you use someone else's chart, diagram, illustration, or photograph, give proper credit.

In summary, selecting an appropriate visual for your purpose is a matter of knowing the strengths and weaknesses of each type of visual. If you want your audience to know facts and figures, a table might be sufficient; however, if you want your audience to make a particular judgment about the data, a bar graph, line graph, or pie chart might be better. If you want to show processes and procedures, diagrams are better than photographs.

The following Reference Window summarizes the strengths of each type of visual for the particular purposes you may have in your presentations. Use this summary to help you decide which visual is appropriate for a particular type of information and purpose.

REFERENCE WINDOW RW

Selecting Appropriate Visuals for Your Purpose

Purpose	Table	Bar graph	Line graph	Pie chart	Flowchart	Organizational chart	Drawing	Photograph	Map
Summarize costs	X	X	X	X					
Relate parts to whole	X				X	X		X	X
Illustrate trends		X	X	X					
Demonstrate cause and effect		X	X						
Compare alternatives	X	X	X	X				X	
Summarize advantages/disadvantages	X								
Provide chronology	X	X	X		X		X		
Follow procedure/work flow					X				
See parts and apparatus	X						X	X	
Explain organization	X					X			
Show spatial relationship							X		X

Selecting **Appropriate Visuals for Your Audience**

Now that you know the purpose of each type of visual, you also need to understand how to choose a visual based on your audience. In analyzing whether a visual is appropriate for a particular audience, a general guideline to follow is that audiences familiar with the topic prefer visuals they can interpret themselves, such as flowcharts, graphs, and diagrams. On the other hand, audiences unfamiliar with the topic need help interpreting the information. Visuals for these audiences should consist of basic tables, graphs, and simple diagrams.

In addition, non-expert audiences generally have a harder time interpreting numerical data than words, so try to avoid numerical visuals. On the other hand, if you can't avoid numerical data, plan to devote extra time during your presentation to explain the numerical data. Likewise, non-expert audiences unfamiliar with certain types of images need additional help interpreting those images. For example, if you show an apparatus, equipment, or machine to non-experts, you must explain in detail what they are seeing and why it's important.

Selecting **Appropriate Visuals for Your Situation**

You not only have to select different visuals for different purposes and audiences, you also have to select visuals based on your situation. Selecting visuals that are appropriate for your situation involves determining which visuals work best for the medium, equipment, and room setup where you'll give your presentation. If the room doesn't have a slide projector or overhead transparency projector, you might find it difficult to use photographs. If you're limited to using a chalkboard, white board, or notepad, you might not have time to create a complex table. In such cases, you might have to provide the complex tables or graphs in posters or handouts. Flowcharts may be effective on a flip chart in a small, well-lit room; however, flip charts aren't effective in a large room, or with large audiences. Maps also are difficult to use in presentations unless they are enlarged or projected, and then they usually need a lot of explanation for the audience to understand them.

No matter which visual you select, be sure everyone in your audience can see, and make sure the medium you use to display the visual enables your audience to understand and correctly interpret your visual.

Now that you've determined which visuals are appropriate for your presentation, you'll need to determine whether you can create them yourself or, need to have someone else create them for you.

Creating **Effective Visuals**

Even though computer programs now make it easier to create visuals, such as graphs and illustrations, you may still need to use a technical illustrator or graphic artist to create specialized diagrams and drawings. In analyzing whether to create visuals yourself or obtain the help of a professional, you should consider what your audience will expect, how much time you have to prepare your visuals, whether you have the expertise and equipment necessary to create the visuals, and whether you have the budget to hire an illustrator or artist.

REFERENCE WINDOW	RW

Questions for Determining Whether You Can Create Visuals Yourself
- What are the expectations for my visuals?
- How much time will I have to prepare the visuals?
- Do I have adequate knowledge or expertise to create the visuals?
- What computer equipment and other production resources do I have available for creating my own visuals?
- How much money is budgeted to hire a technical illustrator or graphic artist?

If you decide to create your own visuals, be aware of the difficulties involved. You should consider the following guidelines (in addition to the suggestions presented earlier for each type of visual):

- Keep your visuals simple. Remember that "less is more" when it comes to creating effective visuals.
- Make your visuals professional-looking. Shabby-looking or amateurish visuals will detract from your presentation and from your credibility.

- Keep your visuals consistent. Keep titles to all of your visuals consistent in size and color so your audience can quickly recognize what your visuals are about.
- Use color sparingly and purposefully. Use the brightest color for the most important information, or to indicate patterns. Don't add color just to make things "look good," or you may end up with something garish.

Of course, one alternative to preparing visuals yourself, or hiring someone to prepare them for you, is to purchase CDs of photographs and clip art, or download images from the Internet. But be aware of copyright laws. As a student, you fall under copyright "fair use" rules, which basically means that you can, for educational purposes only, use copyrighted material on a one-time basis without getting permission from the copyright holder. On the other hand, if you work for a not-for-profit or for-profit company, much stricter copyright laws apply. Learn the copyright laws and abide by them.

Once you've created your visuals or obtained them from some other source, you'll need to plan how to manage and present your visuals during your presentation. The following section will help you understand how to use your visuals.

Making the Most of Your Visuals

Effective visuals can become ineffective if they aren't presented successfully. You'll need to prepare everything beforehand, and then plan how you'll integrate your visuals into your presentation. Perhaps the easiest way to figure out how to present visuals in your presentation is to create a simple storyboard showing the points you want to discuss, and the visual you want to accompany each point.

Using a Storyboard

A **storyboard** is essentially a table or map of instructions and visuals that explains how to complete a process. Storyboards are used in the motion picture industry to map the narrative of a movie with the particular camera shots and special effects that are to accompany that narrative. You can adapt the same storyboarding technique in planning your presentation. Simply take a piece of paper and fold it in half lengthwise. On the left side of the page, briefly describe your presentation point, or write down a heading from your outline. Then on the right side of the page, list or sketch the visual or visuals that you want to accompany that point. You can also include any physical movements or gestures that you want to make, such as pointing to a particular part of a slide or overhead. Figure 2-12 shows a sample storyboard for your presentation at Rocky Mountain State College.

Figure 2-12	STORY BOARD

Benefits of Academic Volunteerism

The first category is Civic Values. Students develop their ability to center on relationships rather than content. They develop an understanding of other cultures and needs, as well as a sense of ethical duty toward society.

Show table listing civic values.

The second category is Professional Development. Students develop problem-solving skills, critical-thinking skills, and writing skills.

Show photo of students performing skills.

The third category is Personal Inspiration. Students develop a sense of who they are and of responsibility for their own actions. They become involved participants rather than just academic observers.

Show table listing types of attributes that students develop.

A storyboard like the one in Figure 2-12 can help you choose and use the best possible visuals for your presentation.

Effectively Presenting Visuals

In addition, you should follow these simple guidelines for effectively presenting your visuals:

- Use visuals to support your ideas, not just as attention getters or gimmicks. Most visuals work best when they supplement your ideas, rather than being tacked on at the beginning or end of your presentation. However, in a formal setting, you should begin your presentation with a slide or overhead showing your name, the title of your presentation, and your company logo.
- Display the visual as you discuss it. Use your storyboard to indicate when you want to display the visual, and then remove the visual when you're through discussing it. Don't let your visuals get ahead or behind of your verbal presentation.
- Stand to the side, not in front, of the visual. Avoid turning your back on your audience as you refer to a visual. Talk directly to your audience, rather than turning toward or talking at the visual.
- Introduce and interpret the visual. Explain to your audience what they should be looking at in the visual and point to what is important. But don't get sidetracked and spend all your time explaining the visual.
- Avoid using too many visuals. Present your material in simple, digestible amounts instead of overwhelming your audience with too much information.
- Turn off the equipment when you're finished.

Figure 2-13 provides a basic worksheet for helping you select appropriate visuals and determining whether you can create them.

Figure 2-13   PRESENTATION VISUALS WORKSHEET

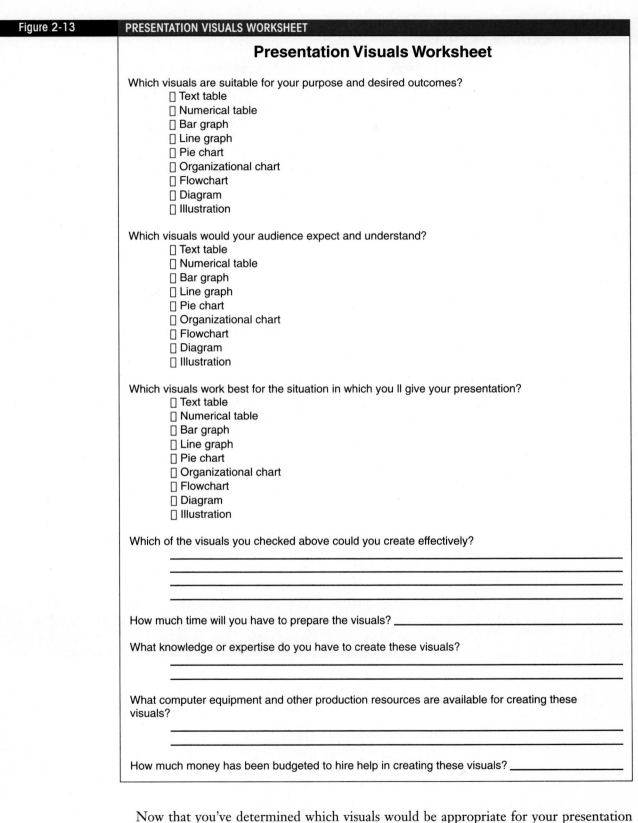

Presentation Visuals Worksheet

Which visuals are suitable for your purpose and desired outcomes?
- ☐ Text table
- ☐ Numerical table
- ☐ Bar graph
- ☐ Line graph
- ☐ Pie chart
- ☐ Organizational chart
- ☐ Flowchart
- ☐ Diagram
- ☐ Illustration

Which visuals would your audience expect and understand?
- ☐ Text table
- ☐ Numerical table
- ☐ Bar graph
- ☐ Line graph
- ☐ Pie chart
- ☐ Organizational chart
- ☐ Flowchart
- ☐ Diagram
- ☐ Illustration

Which visuals work best for the situation in which you ll give your presentation?
- ☐ Text table
- ☐ Numerical table
- ☐ Bar graph
- ☐ Line graph
- ☐ Pie chart
- ☐ Organizational chart
- ☐ Flowchart
- ☐ Diagram
- ☐ Illustration

Which of the visuals you checked above could you create effectively?

_____
_____
_____
_____

How much time will you have to prepare the visuals? _____

What knowledge or expertise do you have to create these visuals?

_____
_____

What computer equipment and other production resources are available for creating these visuals?

_____
_____

How much money has been budgeted to hire help in creating these visuals? _____

Now that you've determined which visuals would be appropriate for your presentation and how to integrate them into your presentation, you're prepared to plan how to deliver your presentation.

Session 2.1 QUICK CHECK

1. Define the purpose for each of the following visuals:
   a. table
   b. graph
   c. chart
   d. illustration

2. Describe a strength and weakness of each of the following visuals:
   a. table
   b. graph
   c. chart
   d. illustrations

3. If you want to show how the number of students in your major has increased in the last five years, which of the following visuals would be appropriate: (a) table, (b) bar graph, (c) line graph, (d) pie chart?

4. If you want to show what percent of your monthly budget goes to housing, which of the following visuals would be appropriate: (a) table, (b) bar graph, (c) line graph, (d) pie chart?

5. If you want to show the managerial structure of your company, which of the following visuals would be appropriate: (a) table, (b) pie chart, (c) organization chart, (d) flowchart?

6. If you want to show the procedure for getting money from an ATM, which of the following visuals would be appropriate: (a) organization chart, (b) flowchart, (c) map, (d) photograph?

7. If you want to show where the Student Senate meets, which of the following visuals would be appropriate: (a) flowchart, (b) map, (c) drawing, (d) photograph?

8. What is a storyboard and how would you use it to make your presentation more effective?

SESSION 2.2

In this session, you'll learn how to: choose an appropriate method for delivering your presentation, overcome your nervousness and improve your delivery, give team presentations, and set up for your presentation.

Choosing an Appropriate Delivery Method

The **delivery method** is your approach for the presentation—written out and read word for word, using a simple outline or notes, or off-the-cuff. Questions you should ask yourself in choosing a delivery method include those that will enable you to determine what is the most appropriate method for your purpose, audience, and situation.

You could present the information you prepared in several different ways. Common delivery methods include

■ written or memorized delivery, reading your entire presentation or repeating it from memory.

■ extemporaneous delivery, giving your presentation from brief notes or an outline.

■ impromptu delivery, speaking without notes and without rehearsal.

Each type of presentation has its own advantages and disadvantages. You should select the delivery method that is appropriate for your purpose, audience, and situation. The following sections will help you determine which type of presentation is best.

Giving a Written or Memorized Presentation

Giving a written or memorized presentation involves completely writing out your presentation and then reading it word for word, or memorizing it in advance.

Figure 2-14	WRITTEN PRESENTATION

Written or memorized presentations are especially effective when you are:

■ unfamiliar with the topic or have a highly complex topic

■ interested in using specific words for persuading or informing your audience

■ addressing a large, unfamiliar, or formal audience

- ■ speaking with a group, or under a strict time limit
- ■ extremely nervous or anxious
- ■ inexperienced in public speaking

Written or memorized presentations don't leave a lot to chance, so they work well in formal settings when you must stick to a topic and stay on time. They're also helpful if you think you'll forget what you prepared, or become nervous and tongue-tied as a result of your inexperience with the topic, or with giving presentations. Written or memorized presentations often are given on certain occasions, such as formal paper sessions at academic or professional conferences.

On the other hand, written or memorized presentations take a long time to prepare, and once you've memorized your presentation, it's not easy to alter it in response to changes in time limits or audience questions. Perhaps the biggest drawback to written or memorized presentations is that it's difficult to sound natural while reading your presentation, or reciting it from memory. So your listeners may lose interest.

For your presentation to the RMSC Student Senate, you're one of several speakers presenting your ideas to the entire Senate. You also have a strict time limit of 12 minutes. In this instance, you want to give a written or memorized presentation so that you can cover everything you want to say in the fewest possible words.

Giving an Extemporaneous Presentation

Extemporaneous presentations involve speaking from a few notes or an outline. Extemporaneous presentations are more flexible than written or memorized presentations, and are ideal for speaking in a more informal setting.

Figure 2-15	EXTEMPORANEOUS PRESENTATION

Extemporaneous presentations are ideal when you are:

- ■ familiar with the topic or audience
- ■ presenting to a medium-sized group, or in an informal setting
- ■ giving a shorter presentation, or have a flexible time limit

- seeking audience participation or questions
- experienced in public speaking

Speaking extemporaneously works well when you're using media requiring no advance preparation, such as chalkboards, white boards, and notepads. An extemporaneous delivery also allows you to have a more natural-sounding presentation, or to adapt your presentation for audience questions or participation.

On the other hand, when you give an extemporaneous presentation, you may have a tendency to go over your time limit, leave out crucial information, or lack precision in explaining your ideas to your listeners. In addition, speaking extemporaneously can make you appear less credible if you have a tendency toward nervousness or anxiety.

Suppose that following your presentation at RMSC, you're asked to speak for 20-30 minutes before a subcommittee of the Student Senate. In that instance, you would probably want to use an extemporaneous delivery so you could speak more naturally and allow members of the subcommittee to ask questions.

Giving an Impromptu Presentation

Impromptu presentations involve speaking without notes, an outline, or memorized text. Impromptu presentations are more flexible than either written, memorized, or extemporaneous presentations; however, they're also more difficult to make effective.

| Figure 2-16 | IMPROMPTU PRESENTATION |

Impromptu presentations work best when you're in the following situations:

- very familiar with your topic and audience
- speaking to a small, intimate group, or in an in-house setting
- asked to speak at the spur of the moment
- more interested in getting the views of your audience than in persuading them

Generally, you should be wary of impromptu presentations because you leave too much to chance. Speaking without notes may result in taking too much time, saying something that offends your audience, or appearing unorganized. If you think you might be asked to speak impromptu, jot down some notes beforehand so you'll be prepared.

Kenna McNaughton, your supervisor, will probably ask you to take 2–3 minutes during the next YES! staff meeting to discuss your presentation at Rocky Mountain State College. You'll want to write down a few notes so you'll be more focused, but you don't need to do extensive planning.

REFERENCE WINDOW				RW
Three Delivery Methods				
Method	**Preparation**	**Audience**	**Situation**	**Strengths**
Written or memorized	Requires much advance preparation	Large	Formal setting; complex or unfamiliar topic; unfamiliar with audience; definite time limit; inexperienced presenter	Effective when exact wording is important; helps overcome nervousness
Extemporaneous	Some advance preparation	Medium, small	Informal setting; familiar with topic and audience; flexible time limit; experienced presenter	Allows more natural presentation; enables audience participation
Impromptu	Little advance preparation, but difficult to give	Small	Informal setting; very familiar with topic and audience; shorter time limits; experienced presenter	Allows flexibility; enables audience participation; spur of the moment

No matter which method of delivery you choose, you'll need to decide whether you want your audience to have an opportunity to ask questions. Preparing for questions from the audience is an important part of giving an effective presentation.

Preparing **for Questions from the Audience**

Some professional speakers suggest that you should savor the idea of questions from the audience, rather than trying to avoid them. The absence of questions, they argue, may actually indicate that your audience had no interest in what you said, or that you spoke too long. Adopting the attitude that interested listeners will have questions enables you to anticipate and prepare for the questions your audience will ask.

Figure 2-17	INTERESTED LISTENERS HAVE QUESTIONS

Things you should consider in preparing for questions include:

- Announce a specific time limit for questions and stick to it. When you want to end, simply state, "We have time for one more question."
- Realize that your audience will ask questions about the information in your presentation that is new, controversial, or unexpected.
- Listen carefully to every question. If you don't understand the question, ask to have it rephrased.
- Repeat the question to make sure everyone in the audience heard it.
- Keep your answers brief. If you need additional time, arrange for it after your presentation.
- If you can't answer a question, admit it, and move on.
- Don't be defensive about hostile questions. Treat every person's question as important and respond courteously.

In your presentation at RMSC, you anticipate that your audience will have questions, such as the following: "What other schools allow their students to receive college credit for working with nonprofits?" "How would a partnership between RMSC and YES! facilitate students receiving credit?" "How would allowing credit for internships affect the number of hours for graduation?" You begin immediately to plan how to answer such questions.

Now that you've determined which type of presentation you want to give, and you're prepared to answer questions from your audience, it's time to think about an almost universal problem—overcoming nervousness.

Overcoming **Nervousness**

Just thinking about speaking in front of other people may cause your heart to beat faster and your palms to sweat. You aren't alone. Feeling nervous about giving a presentation is a natural reaction. But you don't need to let your nervousness interfere with you giving a successful presentation. Being nervous is not all bad, because it means your adrenalin is flowing, and you'll have more energy and vitality for your presentation. In most instances, your nervousness will pass once you begin speaking.

Sometimes, however, nervousness arises from feelings of inadequacy, or from worrying about problems that could occur during a presentation. The best way to overcome these concerns is to carefully plan and prepare your presentation, and then practice it so you can relax and not worry.

Figure 2-18	PLAN, PREPARE, AND PRACTICE

Other things you can do to overcome your nervousness include:

- Focus your presentation on your listeners' needs, not on yourself. When you focus your mind on meeting the needs of your audience, you begin to forget about yourself and how the audience might respond to you.
- Think positively about your presentation. Be optimistic and enthusiastic about your opportunity to gain experience. Visualize yourself as calm and confident.
- Work with your nervousness. Realize that some nervousness is normal and will help make your presentation better. Remember, your audience isn't nearly as concerned about your nervousness as you are.
- Give yourself plenty of time before your presentation. Arrive early to avoid rushing around before your presentation. Devote a few minutes beforehand to relax and review your presentation notes.
- Talk to people beforehand. It's easier to talk to people you know than to complete strangers. If you think of your audience as friends who want you to succeed, you'll gain new confidence in presenting your ideas to them.

- When you first stand up, look at your audience and smile. Then take a few slow breaths to calm yourself before you begin to speak.
- Don't expect everything to be perfect. Have back up plans in case something goes wrong, but handle problems with grace and a sense of humor.
- Observe other presenters. Make a list of the things they do that you like, and try to implement those things into your own presentations.

In preparation for your presentation to the RMSC Student Senate, you decide to meet a few of the Senators beforehand. After meeting a few of the students who represent your class of seniors, you realize that they're concerned with many of the same questions you had, such as how to gain valuable real-world experiences. You realize that they're interested in obtaining helpful information from your presentation that will enable them to make an informed decision in the Student Senate.

Practicing Your Presentation

The most effective way to overcome your nervousness and deliver a smooth presentation is to practice, practice, practice. Begin by simply rehearsing the key points of your presentation in your mind. Then rehearse your presentation in front of a few close friends. Ask your friends what you can do to improve your presentation. Pay special attention to what they say about key aspects of your presentation, such as your introduction, main points, and conclusion. Then rehearse your presentation again.

Figure 2-19	PRACTICING GIVES YOU CONFIDENCE

As you rehearse, use your visual aids and try to speak at the same pace you'll use when giving your presentation. Ask someone to time your presentation. By practicing your presentation until you're comfortable with every aspect of it, you'll go a long way toward reducing the apprehension that comes with feeling unprepared. Practicing your presentation will help you feel more confident as a speaker.

Practicing Your Presentation
- Practice in front of a few friends and a sample of your presentation audience.
- Ask your friends to give you suggestions on how to improve your presentation.
- Time your presentation using the speaking pace you'll use during your presentation.
- Practice with your visual aids.
- Pay particular attention to your introduction, main points, and conclusion.

In an effort to prepare for your presentation to the Student Senate you ask another intern to listen to what you prepared. She says she's not clear on how working with YES! has helped you develop problem-solving skills. You make a note to add another example to support that main point.

The next sections will help you learn how to improve your delivery by establishing eye contact and using a pleasant, natural speaking voice.

Improving Your Delivery

Now matter how well you prepare your presentation, you won't be successful if your delivery is ineffective. No one enjoys a presentation when the speaker refuses to look up, or drones on endlessly in a monotone voice. The best presentations are those where the presenter appears confident and speaks naturally in a conversational manner.

As you practice your presentation, remember to project yourself as a confident and qualified speaker. Two ways that help you appear confident are establishing eye contact with your listeners and speaking in a natural voice.

Establishing Eye Contact

One of the most common mistakes beginners make is failing to establish eye contact with their audience. Speakers who keep their eyes on their notes, stare at their visuals, or look out over the heads of their audience create an emotional distance between themselves and their listeners.

A better method is to look directly at your listeners, even if you have to pause to look up. To establish eye contact, you should look at individuals, not just scan the audience. Focus on a particular member of the audience for just a second or two, then move on to someone else until you eventually get to most of the people in the audience or, if the audience is large, to most parts of the presentation room. You can usually judge how things are going by your audience's reaction, and make adjustments accordingly.

Figure 2-20	ESTABLISH EYE CONTACT

REFERENCE WINDOW   RW

Establishing Eye Contact
- Look directly at your listeners.
- Look at individuals; don't just scan the audience.
- Focus on a particular person, then move on to someone else.
- Eventually look at most of the people or most areas of the audience.

As part of your presentation at RMSC, you'll want to look directly at each member of the Student Senate. That will enable you to create a personal connection with your audience, and see how they're responding to your presentation.

Using a Pleasant, Natural Voice

Most successful presenters aren't blessed with the deep voice of a professional news broadcaster or the rich, full voice of an opera singer; however, they use a pleasant, natural voice to make their presentations more interesting.

Figure 2-21   **USE YOUR NATURAL VOICE**

Consider these suggestions for making your voice more pleasant and appealing:

- Use your natural speaking voice and a conversational manner. Think of talking to your audience as you would to a friend or teacher. That will allow you to use a voice that is more natural and easy to listen to.

- Vary the pitch, rate, and volume of your voice. Overcome monotony by emphasizing important words, pausing at the end of lengthy sentences, and slowing down during transitions. However, don't let the volume of your voice drop at the end of sentences.

- Stand up straight. Improving your posture allows you to project your voice by putting your full strength behind it.

- Learn to relax. Relaxing will improve the quality of your voice by keeping your muscles loose and your voice more natural.

- Practice breathing deeply, which gives you adequate air to speak properly.

Using Proper Grammar and Pronunciation

One of the best ways to be seen as a credible speaker is to use proper grammar and pronunciation. To assure you're pronouncing a word correctly, check its pronunciation in a dictionary. Some common problems in pronunciation include:

- mispronunciations caused by dropping a letter, such as "liberry" instead of library, and "satistics" instead of statistics

- mispronunciations caused by adding a letter or inserting the wrong letter, such as "acrost" instead of across, "learnt" instead of learned, or "stastistics" instead of statistics

- colloquial expressions, such as "crick" instead of creek, or "ain't" instead of isn't or aren't

- lazy pronunciation caused by dropping the final letters, such as "speakin" rather than speaking
- filler words, such as "a," "um," "like," and "ya know."

As part of your presentation to the Student Senate, you wonder how to pronounce the word "data." You look it up in your dictionary and find that the preferred pronunciation is "dāta," not "dăta."

Using **Non-verbal Communication**

Nonverbal communication is the way you convey a message without saying a word. Most nonverbal communication deals with how you use your body to communicate—how you look, stand, and move.

Checking Your Appearance and Posture

Your appearance creates your audience's first impression of you, so make sure your dress and grooming contribute to the total impression you want to convey to your audience. Dress appropriately for the situation, and in a manner that doesn't detract from your presentation.

For your presentation at the RMSC Student Senate, you should wear nicer clothing than you wear to class. This might mean dress slacks and shirt for a man, and a skirt and blouse, or dress, for a woman. For a formal presentation, you should wear business attire, such as a suit and tie for man and a suit or tailored dress for a woman.

| Figure 2-22 | DRESS APPROPRIATELY |

An important part of how you communicate is your posture. Refrain from slouching as your audience may interpret that to mean that you don't care or you're insecure. Stand tall and keep your hands at your side, except to change overheads. Don't bend over or stretch up to speak into the microphone; adjust the microphone for your height.

Using Natural Gestures and Movement

The gestures you use will depend on your personality and your delivery method. It's important to choose gestures that are natural for you, so ask someone else whether your gestures are distracting. Informal presentations lend themselves to more gestures and movement than formal presentations where you're standing in front of a microphone on a podium. But giving a formal presentation doesn't mean you should hide behind the lectern, or behave like a robot. Even formal presentations allow for gestures that are purposeful, spontaneous, and natural.

In your presentation at the RMSC Student Senate, you plan to stand at the podium. But during a staff meeting at YES!, you would stand closer to your coworkers, and would probably be more animated.

Avoiding Annoying Mannerisms

Be aware of your unique mannerisms or recurring movements that can be annoying, such as raising your voice and eyebrows as if you are talking to children; playing with keys, a pen, or equipment; or fidgeting, rocking, and pacing. All of these mannerisms can communicate nervousness, as well as detract from your presentation.

REFERENCE WINDOW		RW
Your Non-verbal Communication		
Eyes	Establish eye contact by looking directly at listeners and focusing on a particular person.	
Voice	Use your natural speaking voice and a conversational manner. Vary the pitch, rate, and volume of your voice. Breathe deeply.	
Appearance and Posture	Stand tall and keep your hands at your side.	
Gestures	Use natural gestures.	
Movement	Avoid recurring movements that can be annoying, and mannerisms, such as rocking and pacing.	

After you practice your presentation to the RMSC Student Senate in front of a friend, she points out that you kept clicking the clip on your pen. You make a note to leave your pen in your backpack during your presentation.

Giving Team or Collaborative Presentations

Giving your presentation as part of a group or team is a common occurrence. Since much of the work in business and industry is collaborative, it's only natural that presentations often are given as a team. The benefits of team presentations include:

■ providing more people with valuable experience. Collaborative presentations involve more people and give each member of a team experience in communicating ideas.

■ providing more workers with exposure and the rewards of a task accomplished.

- allowing for a greater range of expertise and ideas.
- enabling more discussion.
- presenting greater variety in presentation skills and delivery styles.

Figure 2-23   **GIVING TEAM PRESENTATIONS**

A successful team presentation depends on your group's ability to plan thoroughly and practice together. The following suggestions are meant to help you have a successful group presentation:

- Plan for the transitions between speakers.
- Observe time constraints.
- Show respect for everyone and for his or her ideas.
- Involve the whole team in your planning.
- Be sensitive to personality and cultural differences.

Figure 2-24 provides a basic worksheet for practicing and delivering your presentation.

Figure 2-24   PRESENTATION DELIVERY WORKSHEET

Presentation Delivery Worksheet

What delivery method is the most appropriate for your purpose, audience, and situation?
- ☐ Written or memorized delivery chronology
- ☐ Extemporaneous delivery
- ☐ Impromptu delivery

What questions will your audience probably ask?

_____
_____
_____
_____

What are your audience s needs?

_____
_____
_____
_____

What do you enjoy most in a presentation? How can you implement this in your own presentation?

_____
_____
_____
_____

Team Preparation
Transitions between speakers _____
Time allotted for each speaker _____

Rehearsal Checkoff
- ☐ Practiced presentation in front of friends of sample audience
- ☐ Asked friends for suggestions and feedback on presentation
- ☐ Timed your presentation   How long was it? _____
- ☐ Practiced with visual aids
- ☐ Gave particular attention to introduction, main points, and conclusion

Evaluation by Your Target Audience

Established eye contact with audience:	☐ excellent	☐ good	☐ needs improvement
Used natural voice	☐ excellent	☐ good	☐ needs improvement
Used conversational manner	☐ excellent	☐ good	☐ needs improvement
Varied pitch, rate, and volume of voice	☐ excellent	☐ good	☐ needs improvement
Stood up straight	☐ excellent	☐ good	☐ needs improvement
Appeared relaxed	☐ excellent	☐ good	☐ needs improvement
Used proper grammar and pronunciation	☐ excellent	☐ good	☐ needs improvement
Well dressed and groomed	☐ excellent	☐ good	☐ needs improvement
Used natural gestures and movements	☐ excellent	☐ good	☐ needs improvement
Free of annoying mannerisms	☐ excellent	☐ good	☐ needs improvement

Setting Up for Your Presentation

Even the best-planned and practiced presentation can fail if your audience can't see or hear your presentation, or they're uncomfortable. That's why it's important to include the set up for your presentation as an important element of preparation. Of course, there are some things over which you have no control. If you're giving your presentation as part of a professional conference, you can't control whether the room you're assigned is the right size for your audience. Sometimes (but certainly not always) you can't control what projection systems are available, the thermostat setting in the room, or the quality of the speaker system. But you can control many of the things that could interfere with or enhance the success of your presentation, if you consider them in advance.

You've probably attended a presentation where the speaker stepped to the microphone only to find that it wasn't turned on. Or, the speaker turned on the overhead projector to find that the bulb was burned out. Or, the speaker had to wait while the facilities staff adjusted the focus on the slide projector. Much of the embarrassment and lost time can be prevented if the speaker plans ahead and makes sure the equipment works.

| Figure 2-25 | SETTING UP FOR THE PRESENTATION |

But even when the equipment works, it might not work the same as your equipment. One way to prevent this problem is to use your own equipment, or practice in advance with the available equipment. When you must use the available equipment but can't practice with it in advance, you should prepare for the worst and plan ahead.

Here are a few suggestions for planning ahead:

■ Contact the facilities staff before your presentation to make sure they have the equipment you need. Also make sure the equipment is scheduled for the time and place of your presentation.

■ Make sure your equipment is compatible with the facilities at your presentation site. For instance, what version is the software installed on the computer you'll use?

■ Take backup supplies of chalk, markers, and extension cords.

■ If you plan to use visuals requiring a sophisticated projection system, bring along other visuals, such as overhead transparencies or handouts, as a backup in the event that the computer or slide projector fails.

■ If possible, arrive early and test equipment. Allow yourself enough time before your presentation to practice with the equipment and contact technical staff if problems occur.

■ Use a Facilities Checklist to help you anticipate and prevent problems.

Not all of the facilities are under your control. In your presentation at RMSC, you will have access to the facilities staff, but you won't be authorized to change things like temperature settings, or the arrangement of chairs. On the other hand, during your staff meetings at YES!, you can move the chairs away from the table and into a semicircle, or you can adjust the temperature controls to make the room more comfortable.

Using a Facilities Checklist

Using a Facilities Checklist will help you ensure that your audience is comfortable and your equipment works. Planning ahead will also help you prevent many of the problems that may arise. The Facilities Checklist divides the areas you should consider in setting up your presentation into the following categories: room, layout, equipment, and presentation materials. See Figure 2-26.

Figure 2-26	FACILITIES CHECKLIST

Facilities Checklist

Room	☐ Is the room the right size?
	☐ Is the lighting adequate?
	☐ Is the ventilation working properly?
	☐ Is the temperature setting comfortable?
	☐ Are there distracting noises?
Layout	☐ Are the chairs arranged how you want them?
	☐ Are the stand, podium, and microphone set up properly?
	☐ Is the lighting set properly for your type of visuals?
Equipment	☐ Is the electricity on?
	☐ Are there needed extension cords?
	☐ Are all the light bulbs functioning?
	☐ Does the overhead projector, slide projector, or computer projector work properly?
	☐ Is the microphone working with its volume properly adjusted?
	☐ Is the microphone adjusted to the right height?
	☐ Are electrical cords arranged so you don t get entangled in them or trip over them?
	☐ For large presentation rooms, are there microphones set up in the audience for questions and comments, and do they all work properly?
Presentation Materials	☐ Do you have all your visuals (slides, overheads, electronic presentation, handouts, demonstration items)?
	☐ Do you have a pointer?
	☐ If you re using a laser pointer, is it working properly?
	☐ Is a tripod available for your poster or notepad?
	☐ Are there thumbtacks, pins, or tape for your poster or sign?
	☐ Are your slides properly loaded into the slide projector carousel or slide tray?
	☐ Do you have a chalkboard, white board, or notepad?
Supporting Services	☐ Do you have drinking water?
	☐ Does the audience have notepaper and pens?
	☐ Does the entrance to the presentation room give information about the speaker or session being held there?
	☐ Do you know how to handle audiovisual, lighting, or sound problems in the event something goes wrong?

In considering the room in which you'll give your presentation, you'll want to check whether the room is properly ventilated, adequately lighted, and free from distracting noises, such as clanking of dishes in the kitchen, hammering and sawing by work crews, or interference from the speakers in adjacent rooms.

In considering the layout of the room, you'll want to make sure the chairs are arranged so that everyone in the audience can see and hear your presentation. You'll also want to make sure the microphone stand provides enough room for your notes, or that the equipment, such as the overhead projector, is close enough that you won't have to walk back and forth to your notes.

In considering the equipment, you'll want to check to make sure all the needed equipment is available and functioning properly. You'll also want to make sure you have adequate space for your equipment and access to electrical outlets. You might want to make arrangements for extra bulbs for the projector or overhead, or bring your own.

In considering the presentation materials, you'll want to make sure that you have chalk or markers for the chalkboard and white board, an easel to support your visuals, or thumbtacks you can use to mount your visuals on the wall or a poster board. You'll also want to make sure you have a glass of water in case your throat gets dry.

As you go through the Facilities Checklist, you find that everything you need is available in your presentation room at Rocky Mountain State College. You feel confident knowing that you have done everything possible on your part to prepare for your presentation. When the presentation time comes, you deliver your message with a natural, clear voice, and keep eye contact with your audience. Your audience responds favorably to your presentation, asks meaningful questions for which you are prepared, and compliments you on a job well done. Your presentation is a success in every way.

Session 2.2 QUICK CHECK

1. List and define three common presentation delivery methods.

2. Which delivery method(s) are appropriate if you must speak under a strict time limit and want to use specific wording in your presentation?

3. Which delivery method(s) are appropriate if you're asked to speak on the spur of the moment?

4. Which delivery method(s) are appropriate if you want audience participation?

5. True or False. You should avoid questions from the audience because it shows that your audience didn't pay attention to your presentation.

6. List the most important way to overcome nervousness about giving a presentation.

7. Define non-verbal communication and give one example.

8. Give an example of a filler word you should avoid in your presentation.

REVIEW ASSIGNMENTS

Tanner Granatowski is an intern for Business With a Heart, another nonprofit organization in the Colorado Springs area. Business With a Heart matches people willing to donate goods, time, or talents with those in desperate need. The non profit company also partners with local businesses to distribute goods, similar to food banks. You're asked to help Tanner prepare and give three presentations for Business With a Heart.

The first presentation will be a 20-minute presentation to members of the local Chamber of Commerce (approximately 40 people). Your purpose in this presentation is to inform the Chamber of the goals and purposes of Business With a Heart. The presentation will take place in the large banquet hall of the new Colorado Springs City Center, which is fully equipped with the latest technology.

The second presentation will be a 10-minute presentation to 10 members of the Board of Directors of The Henderson Foundation, a national foundation that gives money to non-profit organizations. Your purpose in this presentation is to persuade the Board of Directors to donate $400,000 to help Business With a Heart expand its programs. The presentation will take place in the 100-year-old foundation board room. It has electricity, but no computer projection equipment.

The third presentation will be a 40-minute presentation to five members of the staff at Business With a Heart. Your purpose in this presentation is to show staff members how to contact local business owners over the phone to find out if they are interested in donating their excess goods. The presentation will take place in a small staff room. Do the following:

1. Explain the differences and similarities between the three presentations in terms of your audience. Complete an Audience Analysis Worksheet for each presentation.

2. Explain how your purpose and the type of information you will present in each presentation will affect the visuals that you would use.

3. Explain the differences and similarities between the three presentations in terms of the presentation situation. Complete a Situation and Media Assessment Worksheet for each presentation.

4. Explain how your purpose and the type of information you will be presenting in each of these presentations will affect the visuals that you use. Complete a Presentation Visuals Worksheet for each presentation.

5. Give an example of how you would use a numerical table in one presentation.

6. Give an example of how you would use a graph in one presentation.

7. Give an example of how you would use a chart in one presentation.

8. Give an example of how you would use an illustration in one presentation

9. Explain how your purpose, audience, and situation would affect the delivery method you would use for each presentation. Complete a Presentation Delivery Worksheet for each presentation.

10. Create a storyboard showing an idea and visual for one presentation.

11. List two questions you think the audience might ask for each presentation.

12. Give an example of how your nervousness might vary for the presentations. Explain what you would do to overcome your nervousness.

13. Describe what you would wear for each presentation.

14. Using the Facilities Checklist, describe one aspect you can control and one you can't control for each presentation.

CASE PROBLEMS

Case 1. Wyoming ESCAPE Wyoming ESCAPE is a Jackson Hole-based company that plans corporate retreats, taking advantage of Wyoming's beautiful scenery and recreation. Wyoming ESCAPE provides activities to help harried workers and executives unwind and play team-enhancing games—everything from ropes courses to river raft races in the summer, and snowman building and cross-country skiing in the winter. The staff at Wyoming ESCAPE asks you to help them prepare for three presentations.

The first presentation will be a 20-minute presentation to sales personnel (approximately 15 people). Your purpose in this presentation is to inform the sales staff about the activities you provide so that they can market the retreats. The presentation will take place at company headquarters in a large conference room. The conference room does not have a computer projection system, but does have a slide projector.

The second presentation will be a 10-minute presentation to approximately 45 potential participants. Your purpose in this presentation is to persuade your audience to consider Wyoming ESCAPE for their corporate retreat, and to contact your sales staff for further details. The presentation will take place at a national human resources conference in the ballroom of a large hotel. The hotel has a computer projection system, as well as a slide projector.

The third presentation will be a 40-minute presentation to five staff members who'll conduct the activities. Your purpose in this presentation is to demonstrate how to conduct several new activities that will be used during corporate retreats. The presentation will take place in a small conference room. There is no slide projector or computer projection system in the conference room, but there is a large white board.

Do the following:

1. Complete a Purpose and Outcomes Worksheet for each presentation.

2. Explain the differences and similarities between the audiences for the three presentations, including any general demographics that you can determine. Complete an Audience Analysis Worksheet for each presentation.

3. Explain how the settings for these presentations would probably affect your audience's expectations and the appropriate level of formality.

4. Determine appropriate and inappropriate media for each presentation. Complete a Situation and Media Assessment Worksheet for each presentation.

5. Complete a Focus and Organization Worksheet to determine an appropriate organizational pattern and organize the text in your presentation accordingly.

6. Explain how your purpose, audience, and setting would affect the visuals you would use. Complete a Presentation Visuals Worksheet for each presentation.

7. Give an example of a visual you could use to show sales personnel that the number of participants has decreased in the last year.

8. Give an example of a visual you could use to convince potential participants that they would enjoy attending Wyoming ESCAPE.

9. Give an example of a visual you could use to show the staff a new game for the retreat.

10. Create a storyboard showing an idea and visual for one presentation.

11. Using a Presentation Delivery Worksheet, specify which delivery method you would use for each presentation, and list one question you think the audience might ask for each presentation. Also explain how your level of nervousness might differ for each presentation, and what you would do to overcome your nervousness.

12. Using a Facilities Checklist for each presentation, list two set up details you would want to check for each presentation.

Case 2. FamilyOrigins.com   Tamar Ruest works for FamilyOrigins.com, a company that allows family members to speak to each other free-of-charge over the Internet, share stories and photographs through personal Web pages, and obtain genealogy-related supplies over the Internet, such as government reports, printed family histories, and forms for creating a family tree. You're asked to create three presentations.

The purpose of the first presentation is to inform your listeners of the success of FamilyOrigins.com. Your presentation will be given to 50 attendees at a genealogy conference held in a large conference room in a local motel. There is no computer projection system or slide projector available at the motel, but your company has an overhead projector you could take to the conference.

The purpose of the second presentation is to persuade your audience of the need for genealogy. Your audience consists of 15 members of your family (or someone else's) attending a family reunion held at an outdoor pavilion at a local state park. There is an electrical outlet at the pavilion, but no slide projector, computer projection system, or blackboard.

The third presentation, demonstrating how to download the form to create a family tree, will be given to your classmates. You should base your media selection upon the facilities at your school and classroom.

Do the following:

1. Complete a Purpose and Outcomes Worksheet for each presentation.

2. Explain the differences and similarities between the above three groups in terms of their age, level of education, and familiarity with the subject. Complete an Audience Analysis Worksheet for each presentation.

3. Explain how the settings for these presentations would affect your audience's expectations and the appropriate level of formality. Complete a Situation and Media Assessment Worksheet for each presentation.

4. Determine appropriate and inappropriate media for each presentation.

5. Complete a Focus and Organizational Worksheet to determine an appropriate organizational pattern and organize the text in your presentation accordingly.

6. Explain how your purpose, audience, and setting for each presentation would affect the visuals you would use.

7. Complete a Presentation Visuals Worksheet for each presentation, giving an example of an appropriate visual for each presentation.

8. Create a storyboard showing an idea and visual for one presentation.

9. Using a Presentation Delivery Worksheet, identify which delivery method you would use for each presentation. List two questions you think the audience might ask for each presentation. Explain how your level of nervousness might differ for each presentation, and what you would do to overcome your nervousness.

10. Complete a Facilities Checklist for each presentation, determining two things you should check for each presentation.

Case 3. Kids Kreative Communication Kids Kreative Communication sells fairy tale and nursery rhyme software for teaching young children to read, including online coloring books and stories that use a particular child's name. You're asked to give some presentations for Kids Kreative.

The purpose of the first presentation is to demonstrate how a particular software program works. Your audience will be five elementary school teachers who will use the software at a local elementary school. Your presentation will be given in the school's computer classroom, which has a white board and a computer projection system.

The purpose of the second presentation is to interest approximately 40 elementary school principals attending a national teaching convention in the complete line of Kids Kreative software. Your presentation will be given in a hotel conference room which has an overhead projector and a slide projector.

The purpose of the third presentation is to inform 10 programmers at Kids Kreative of some of the needs of current software users. Your presentation will be given at Kids Kreative headquarters, in a small conference room which has an overhead projector and a white board.

Do the following:

1. Complete a Purpose and Outcomes Worksheet for each presentation.

2. Explain the differences and similarities between the above three groups in terms of their age, level of education, and familiarity with the subject. Complete an Audience Analysis Worksheet for each presentation.

3. Explain how the settings for these presentations would affect your audience's expectations and the appropriate level of formality. Complete a Situation and Media Assessment Worksheet for each presentation.

4. Determine appropriate and inappropriate media for each presentation.

5. Complete a Focus and Organization Worksheet to determine an appropriate organizational pattern, and organize the text in your presentation accordingly.

6. Explain how your purpose, audience, and setting for each presentation would affect the visuals you would use. Complete a Presentation Visuals Worksheet for each presentation.

7. Create a storyboard showing an idea and a visual for one presentation.

8. Using a Presentation Delivery Worksheet, specify which delivery method you would use for each presentation. List one question you think the audience might ask for each presentation. Explain how your level of nervousness might differ for each presentation, and what you would do to overcome your nervousness.

9. Complete a Facilities Checklist for each presentation, determining which items on the checklist would apply to each presentation.

Case 4. Flores High Performance Seminars Juanita Flores owns Flores High Performance Seminars, a company providing monthly seminars and training on coaching, leadership, teambuilding, and presentations. Juanita asks you to give a presentation to your class on one of these topics. Working with another member of the class, create a 5-7 minute presentation for your classmates. Do the following:

1. Decide what type of presentation you'll give.

2. Complete a Purpose and Outcomes Worksheet for your presentation.

3. Define your audience according to their general demographic features of age, gender, level of education, and familiarity with your topic. Complete an Audience Analysis Worksheet for your presentation.

4. Assess the situation for your presentation by describing the setting and size of your audience. Complete a Situation and Media Assessment Worksheet.

5. Select appropriate media for your presentation and explain why they are appropriate.

6. Complete a Focus and Organization Worksheet and organize the text in your presentation accordingly.

7. Show two ways you could focus your presentation and limit the scope of your topic.

8. Select a method for gaining your audience's attention, and write an introduction using that method.

9. Create an advance organizer or overview for your presentation.

10. Identify at least two sources for information on your topic and consult those sources.

11. Select an appropriate organizational pattern for your presentation.

12. Identify four transitional phrases that you'll use in your presentation.

13. Write a summary for your presentation recapping the key ideas.

14. Complete a Presentation Visuals Worksheet.

15. Create an appropriate visual for your presentation.

16. Using the Presentation Delivery Worksheet, decide on an appropriate presentation style. Write a list of questions you think your classmates will ask.

17. Practice your presentation in front of another group in your class, and ask them to complete the evaluation part of the Presentation Delivery Worksheet.

18. Complete a Facilities Checklist for your presentation.

19. Set up your classroom.

20. Give your presentation to your classmates.

QUICK CHECK ANSWERS

Session 2.1

1. (a) organize information in horizontal rows and vertical columns (b) show the relationship of two variables along a horizontal and a vertical axis (c) show the relationship of variables without using a coordinate system (d) show relationships that aren't numerical

2. (a) table (strengths): effective for making facts and details accessible, organizing data by categories, summarizing results and recommendations, and comparing sets of data; table (weaknesses): not effective for showing change across time, trends, procedures, or spatial relationships. (b) graph (strengths): effective for comparing one quantity to another, showing changes over time, and indicating patterns or trends; graph (weaknesses): not effective for showing organizational hierarchy, procedures or work flow, parts and wholes, or spatial relationships. (c) chart (strengths): effective for comparing parts to the whole, explaining organizations, and showing chronology, procedures, and work flow; chart (weaknesses): not effective for showing changes over time or percentages. (d) illustration (strengths): effective for showing how things appear, the assembly and relationship of parts and processes to each other, and spatial relationships; illustration (weaknesses): not effective for summarizing data, providing chronology, or showing processes.

3. a., b., and c.
4. d.
5. c.
6. b.
7. b., c., and d.
8. technique from movie industry showing dialogue and accompanying camera shots and special effects; list idea you're discussing on left side of sheet and the accompanying visual on the right side of the sheet.

Session 2.2

1. written or memorized presentation—write out presentation and read it word for word or memorize it; extemporaneous presentation—speak from a few notes or outline; impromptu presentation—speak without notes or outline, or off-the-cuff.
2. written or memorized presentation
3. impromptu presentation
4. extemporaneous presentation, impromptu presentation
5. False; questions probably mean your audience listened and was interested in what you had to say.
6. planning, preparation, and practice
7. conveying a message without talking; appearance, posture, body movement, gestures, and mannerisms.
8. "uh," "um," "you know," "er," "a," "like"

DATE DUE
